Life on Limestone

Life on Limestone

Poetry and Prose by Anna Adams
Watercolours by Norman Adams

First published in 1994 by
Smith Settle Ltd
Ilkley Road
Otley
West Yorkshire
LS21 3JP

ISBN Paperback 1 85825 035 8
ISBN Hardback 1 85825 036 6

British Library Cataloguing-in-Publication Data: A catalogue record is available for this book from the British Library.

Designed, printed and bound by
SMITH SETTLE
Ilkley Road, Otley, West Yorkshire LS21 3JP

Acknowledgements

Acknowledgements are due to the following papers and magazines where some of the prose and poetry in this book made their first appearances: *Guardian, Countryman, Craven Herald, PN Review, Acumen, Encounter, Pennine Platform, Orbis, Green Book* and *Yorkshire Journal;* and to BBC Radio 3 and Radio Leeds for broadcasting some of this material.

Thanks are due to John Killick for advice and encouragement.

Contents

Dedicated to the memory of Guy Barton

Moral Support

When I was a child at home there was, on my parents' shelves, an unattractive dirty-green book labelled, in dull gold lettering on its spine, *Walden*, by Thoreau. In searching for reading matter I used to avoid this book, thinking, when I first noticed it, that it was about a German person or place by a Frenchman, and, whatever language it may have been written in, it would certainly be dull. The book had a Victorian look about it, and it wasn't a novel, so it would contain no Dostoevskian abysses of the human heart into which I might peer; nor had it any pictures. By the time I had inherited most of my father's books, including this one, I had quite often come across quotations from Thoreau, and I had always enjoyed them, but I still postponed the reading of *Walden*, as I imagined it to be an endless nature notebook; and though nature is fine, mankind is finer, I thought, echoing Keats.

But at last I have taken the book down from the shelf where it has been jammed in for so long. Possibly I was intending to dust it, but I have been reading it instead. It is true that, physically, it is an uninspiring little volume — a member of the 'Walter Scott' library, 'bound in cloth with uncut edges and gilt top, price 1/6'. It was probably printed and bound in the 1880s, although the only dated inscription on its flyleaf says 'Eva Wright from Blanche, February 1899'. Another says 'Percy from Bert', and this may have been the first. The third inscription is my father's name in his own handwriting, along with evidence that he actually read the book, for there is a list, in pencil, of unfamiliar words that he had stumbled over and noted in order to look them up later. 'Suent', 'amnesty' and 'freshet', are among them. The others are illegible.

But all this has very little to do with Thoreau, who is, by the magic of the written word, compressed between the pages of this dingy little book which has passed from long-dead hand to long-dead hand until it has reached this, my temporarily living one. He is not in the pages of the book as a pressed plant might be. He is far from dried up and mummified; he is still very much alive, though dead for a hundred years. He sits and thinks all morning long by the waters of Walden Pond, and we can sit inside his head and share his thoughts. The pond, too, is preserved in the yellowing pages, in all its blue-green translucence. There are the shoals of fish, the swaying weeds, the loons, wild ducks and geese that swim on its surface. The reflections of trees standing about it still stab its depths. The wakes of pond skaters and water beetles wrinkle its surface on still midsummer days. It freezes, winter long, and there is Thoreau, out on the ice, cutting a hole to drop his fishing-line through. We can hear the ice cracking in the intense frost.

This miracle of preservation is worked by Thoreau's prose, which is as clear as his mind, which is, in its turn, as clear as Walden's waters; so through it we can see anything he wishes us to see, including the man himself. There he is at the door of his cabin, sitting in the spring sunshine and reading the *Bhagavadgita.*

He claims to do the minimum amount of work necessary in order to remain alive without growing rich. He cultivated a field of beans, and philosophised about this activity, and wrote down his thoughts and sensations so that we can both understand his ideas and feel the sun-warmed earth as he hoed it. We can smell the sap of the cut weeds. He fished in Walden Pond. He baked his own bread in his hand-made house in the woods. He lived in this house through the first summer of its existence, before it was completely finished, so that there were gaps between the fragrant pine logs, and he described himself as being caged up beside the birds. He would walk home through the woods from visiting Emerson in Concord, and we can walk with him, if we wish, as passengers in his mind.

He writes about the Indians with respect and understanding. He writes about economics from a very revolutionary point of view. The problem, as he sees it, is not how to become rich, but how to remain poor. Riches and fine houses he sees as burdens; technological progress he sees as slavery. 'Men have become the tools of their tools', he says in a pithily aphoristic paragraph. After discussing beautiful houses and beautiful works of art, he finishes by saying: 'a taste for the beautiful is best cultivated out of doors, where there is no house and no housekeeper.' He saw man as a 'sojourner in nature', and felt that man should remain aware that he stood on the bare earth, and that forgetfulness of this fact tends to man's downfall.

Reading Thoreau encourages me in my own wavering beliefs.

Everyone has become so urban, nature is so old-fashioned and repetitive; the voice of doubt suggests that to live in the country, to write about the country, to walk in the fields and creep along the hedges peering into birds' nests and noticing flowers, is to be an anachronism. Twentieth-century man is urban, technological man. Farms are factories. Foods are vitamins. Vitamins are pills. Plastic flowers never die; and they can be splashed with laboratory perfume. One can pass through life without ever touching the ground. Nature need not come into the picture. Insecticides will keep it out. And so on. Yet the fact remains that, in spite of all the propaganda, I do not feel thoroughly alive unless I am in contact with wild nature. In Battersea I never knew what time of year it was; I felt lost in time: and Thoreau backs me in my groping belief that we must live on the ground and not be insulated from the grass.

In cities people may produce urban art and urban poetry in response to their experiences, but they are in a secondary or tertiary situation, and their senses, therefore, are less alive to the primary situation of man, which is on the ground, surrounded by the other creatures in their living habitat, and wound about by the sun and moon as they and we go on our endless way through the vast and mysterious dark. All man's other situations are within the context of this one, and if this relationship is destroyed then all the towers and palaces, the libraries and other boxed delights, must disintegrate.

There was much that seemed important to the little town of Concord in the mid-nineteenth century. Very few people now know what it was, and most of the little that is known seems faintly ridiculous. Thoreau saw what was really important, and what was important for him then is still important for us today; and what he saw as important was the quality of human life.

'If we do not get out sleepers and forge rails', he said, 'and devote days and nights to the work, but go tinkering upon our lives to improve them, who will build railroads? And if railroads are not built, how shall we get to heaven in season? But if we stay at home and mind our business, who will want railroads? We do not ride on the railroad, it rides upon us.' (For railroad read motorway.) And elsewhere Thoreau says: 'I have travelled much in Concord'. It is this — staying at home and minding our business, and travelling much in Horton-in-Ribblesdale — that I need moral support to write about. When the world is full of terrible events (that I am helpless to do anything more than wring my hands over), and Great and Important events, how can I have the face to write about nothing in particular in nowhere in particular? Yet the world is roughly spherical in shape, so that no part of its surface is elevated much above any other part, and all places are equally far from the centre. The earth is, in short, a very democratic shape, and every square inch of its surface should be equal. I may be making a virtue of necessity, but Here and Now are all that I can know anything about, and the place where I live is as important to me as New York's heart (if it has one) may be to rather a large number of other people. I can only write about what I know and care about, hoping that perception makes things remarkable, and caring makes them important.

Snowsickness

It started to snow on the evening of Christmas Day, and we were pleased because we had just given the children a toboggan each; and what is the good of toboggans without snow? So on the fine frosty days after Christmas the children, the toboggans and the snow played together during most of the short period of daylight.

It looked very pretty, this first light snowfall which picked out all the ledges on the crags and emphasised the vertical pattern of trees on the steep white hillsides. We felt as though we were living in a Durer engraving. But then the great Siberian wind-machine sent hurricanes of icy, breath-baffling wind which lasted for days on end. The fields appeared to smoke, as though the snow were white-hot ash, and blown snow drifted before the wind until checked by the stone walls, when it broke over them like waves and fell on the leeward side in fantastic heaps. This wind-carved sculpture grew and grew, spreading over roads and fields, burying sheep, motorcars, and people if it could get them, until it had obliterated our familiar landscape and created a new one: a white wilderness of cold ash-heaps.

As each false thaw was succeeded by new blizzards, I began to feel both metaphorically and literally sick of the snow, for there is such a thing as snowsickness. To walk about in the crisp, sugary landscape became like walking on the surface of an inedibly vast iced cake. The banks of snow by the road, which had started to thaw and sag, and then frozen again into floppy-formed but hard heaps, looked to me like too much meringue, or whipped cream. And in the late afternoons the sun went down to the south-west like a luminous raspberry fruitdrop, its pink light transforming Pen-y-Ghent, our local mountain, into a mound of strawberry ice-cream.

I found, by comparing notes with other people, that this sensation of snowsickness is quite common; it has something to do with the whiteness of the snow dazzling the eyes, and in some mysterious way affecting the stomach.

'Siberian' became a word that was much bandied about. Out shopping one morning, having heard the suave-voiced weatherman on the radio use it for about the twelfth time, I met the exiled Polish lady who lives in our village.

'How does this compare with Siberia?' I asked her, for she has been, very involuntarily, to that fabled place.

'Oh this is nothing', she said. 'In Archangel forest, sometimes, it was fifty degrees below freezing, and you had to be very careful, for often, after you had been out only ten minutes, your cheeks and nose would go white, and quick! you must rub them with snow, for else they will be frostbitten off. And sometimes we were working in the forestry up to the waist in snow. And only two of my whole family got out of it alive you know. First my stepfather, and then the small children, and then my mother died. She was only thirty-eight, and if she were alive now she would not be sixty. We lived, my sister and I, by selling our dead parents' boots and the children's clothes.'

After a silence: 'This is nothing', she said again, indicating the death-white fields, black-edged with walls.

The snow became depressing. The dust-sheeted landscape seemed to be abandoned by life for good. I sat indoors while the wind whined round the house and flurries of snow hissed past the window like an endless succession of sighing ghosts. Lean hares came into the garden, their fur caked with ice, and they nibbled at the stalks of the roses and whatever debris of last summer still jutted above the snow. I felt very honoured to have such wild guests, and took out cabbage leaves for them, but they always bolted, in a drunken and staggery way, coming back later to ignore my offerings and to continue to gnaw at the tough wallflower stalks and other such dry bones of dead vegetation.

Then, for two days in succession, the air was mild. The wind blew from the south-west and the weatherman on the radio spoke confidently of a thaw. The heaps of snow dwindled and shrank; water dripped from gutters and gurgled down drains. Under trees, the soft snow was pitted by the dripping of the thaw. Starlings perched on the trees and did impersonations of curlews' love-calls, conjuring up visions of the spring. I walked out over the fields where the threadbare sheet of snow was rapidly wearing into bigger and bigger holes. And through the holes I saw the grass.

'This is it', I thought, 'this is the end. Now spring will begin.'

On the way home I met Mark, the roadman, who leant on his shovel while his leathery face, creased by fifty years of mirth at his own tall stories, beamed complacently, as though he personally were responsible for the thaw.

'I've cleared this road to Brackenbottoms eleven times', he said.

The following day he found himself clearing it for the twelfth time, for the icy winds from Europe had the upper hand once more. Returning from taking my children to school through the newly formed canyons of snow, I met him and his happy though futile band of shovellers, their donkey-jackets feathery with big flakes, going home defeated by the still-raging blizzard. And a day or two later, when the wind had dropped, I met them again, tackling bigger drifts than ever.

'You should have seen me last night', said Mark. 'I was up on the house roof shovelling snow out of the chimney to let the smoke out. Then this morning we had to fetch the Fire Brigade from Settle to bring a ladder before we could get up onto that drift to start cutting it.'

'Do you employ women?' I asked.

'Anyone at all', said Mark: 'men, women or hermaphrodites.'

'Well, if you are still shovelling on Monday I will come and join you', I said, and I meant it, stupid though it is to expend so much energy on repeatedly shovelling the unlimited supplies of snow instead of going quietly home to hibernate until it melts away of its own accord.

Snowdrifts

Having been away for a few days, I returned to find that the elements had left great mounds of what appeared, in the evening half-light, to be a delivery of National Dried Bathwater to store for use in time of drought, for snow lay in deep drifts about the house. It was no longer very cold, and we do not have a refrigerated cellar, so the snow couldn't stay. It was already mushy like wet sugar, and sank down, dwindling hourly, turning to water that trickled and glistened about the saturated ground.

'This is nothing', said the children. 'The school bus couldn't get through on Wednesday — we had a day off school. The lane was filled right up, and that rowan tree was buried so that only the top half of its branches stuck up out of the snow, like whiskers. The trunk was quite buried.' They had obviously enjoyed it. 'It was as high as this — ' said everyone, holding their hands above their heads.

Days later, though the thaw continued, and it was warm enough for the air to be full of hovering flies, the hillsides were still gashed with the pattern of jagged white drifts, like patches of sea foam where a great wave of weather had smashed. On either side of every wall ran thick white banks of snow, greatest on the north side. Looking up-valley on Saturday afternoon, little red and black footballers ran about in the drizzle between two of the horizontal white ribbons of snow that marked the walls of level riverside fields.

On the south side of Horton Scar a great bank of snow sagged and crumpled as it wasted away from underneath, and deep-voiced waterfalls of melted snow poured into the overflowing brown pools.

After more than a week of thaw, our drifts are now as small and flat as sad bits of washing blown from the line in a gale, grown muddy while waiting for rescue and re-washing. Yet they are white again in their new incarnations — as waterfalls, and rapids of snow-water in the Ribble; as the white mists that drift about, veiling and unveiling Pen-y-Ghent; and as the snowdrops pushing up through the dead leaves on the floor of the wood by Douk Ghyll.

Even though more snow comes, the great white sheets on the fields do not stay long enough to accumulate the journalism of disaster — footprints of fox and hare, the arrow prints of hungry birds, the trampling of sheep about a scattered bale of hay — but they are quickly pulped and repiaced by the poetry of the grass.

The Carpet-Slippered Hare

Dotted and dashed, the indiscreet
snow broadsheet tells the news
in Morse tapped out by long back feet
and ladylike front paws;
'The carpet-slippered hare grows desperate
for straws.'

Gnawing our cabbage to its root,
(dropped pellets pay the bill),
he hobbles off, no longer fleet,
finds nothing left to fill
his belly, levers himself— hunger-light—
uphill.

While proley rabbits crowd in holes,
aloof but down-and-out
Hare sits on fitted carpet soles
for comfort. Delicate
front paws scratch snow for grass, but blizzard seals
his fate.

Hissing and whispering, the sleet—
past flattened ears, dim eyes—
flies horizontal, cakes his coat,
but ice lacks calories;
so Hare falls off his ill-assorted feet
and dies.

Laughing, the undertaker crows
dismember him, and eat;
but on the piebald hill grass grows
more green as snows retreat.
There, cantering on well-heeled slipper-toes,
Hares meet.

Moorland Landscape (1960)

Worm

This drizzle rots white tapes
of wallside snow, thaws out
the earth so that a worm escapes

to probe, with tapered snout,
hard tarmac where it cannot find —
although it gropes about —

the way back underground.
It stretches out its span
of pearl-complexioned, blind

and naked gut, grows thin
and long, and then contracts
its length again.

It seems the fool elects
to cross the rain-wet road
while ignorant of facts

such as: it is thrush-food,
and there are tractor-wheels.
Misguided annelid,

you seem to have two tails
but one's your brainless head.
Unminded grit-canals

should hide beneath the mud:
why not move in reverse
and thus go back to bed

before your plight grows worse?
Its boneless finger points
across a universe

of road, so, all at once
I seize the creature's saddle.
Convulsed, and lacking joints,

it knots into a muddle
which I set down on grass.
Released from its tight huddle

it burrows. Soon its arse
waves me goodbye, withdraws
to worms' nutritious house:

the home of both of us.

Pen-y-Ghent from the south-east (1961)

Summer in Winter

Now, in the very small hours of the year, February on the calendar being equivalent to 2 am on the clock, although it is not at all unlikely that winter has a big white surprise saved up for us, we find ourselves expecting the spring. But it is a waste of time, even of wintertime, not to live in the present, and perhaps it is easier to appreciate winter if we seek out the mid-winter summers that are going on. It is not only in the antipodes that it is summer now; right under our noses — on rocks, walls and tree-roots — forests of moss and cities of lichen are enjoying their growing season. Revived by the cold and wet, old tufts of moss send out tentacles that feel their way over walls like hairy green caterpillars. They find and colonise naked stones, covering them with new green wigs. Moss grows like mountain forests on the ledges of drystone walls, and it clothes tree-boles in green fur-coats, while ash-grey lichens spread over stones like smouldering fires, often leaving a burnt-out centre, thus forming rings. There are also crinkled scabs of yellow lichen, and whitish crusts that erect dusty trumpets, all luxuriating in the misty drizzle.

But if we can find no comfort in the fact that even in the dead of winter the mosses and lichens are having a ball, there is also the mineral botany of frost which may come into season any night now. We are all familiar with the moonfronds that grow on windowpanes. There is also ice-moss that grows over walls, the daggers and dragons' teeth that shoot in water before it freezes solid, and, up on the fells, last summer's desiccated sedges bristling with needles of ice like ferocious glass cacti. There can be crystal ferns and glittering ice-flowers everywhere.

If even all this cannot make us rejoice in winter for winter's sake, then there is the best-dressed rock in Ribblesdale, green throughout the year with ferns, mosses, cranesbill, herb-Robert and even nettles, in the sheltered amphitheatre of Douk Ghyll scar. While plodding across muddy fields in the rain in order to see it, we may notice that the rooks are flying about with twigs in their beaks, rebuilding their shanty-town in the trees. Already they are family-planning. And spreading crowds of snowdrops are white, by the beck. They stand meekly awaiting the sun while, although we live nine hundred feet above sea-level, aconites are humping themselves backwards out of the soil and showing their shining faces in the garden.

White Blackbirds

We had been showing some of the sights of Yorkshire to my son's school-friend from Manchester, and we emerged from the historic gloom of Skipton Castle in the late afternoon of a February day. Behind us, the oppressive walls enclosed comfortless rooms, fighting-chambers with arrow-slots, the comic long-drop privy, a terrible dungeon, and that ancient tree that has been imprisoned for three hundred years in the Conduit Court. It sighs continuously, like the sea, for all past prisoners whose lives were extinguished within these walls. As we stood at the foot of the entrance flight of stone stairs, we heard the unmistakeable song of a blackbird rejoicing in earliest spring, and freedom.

Looking about us for the origin of the song, we saw, perched on a roof-ridge, a blackbird with a white head. Perhaps this whiteness was a trick of the light; and possibly the feathers shone because a white ray from the declining sun shot like an arrow through a chink in the clouds, and struck the bird. So we looked very carefully, and it really did have a white head, like a judge's wig, extending a little way over its shoulders on either side.

As we went through the cave-like darkness of the gateway, the gatekeeper would have told us about Normans subduing Saxons, invading Scots burning down the earliest castle, the additions of each age to the building, the subtractions of Cromwell, Lady Anne Clifford's restoration, and her planting of the yew tree in the court; but I wanted to know if he knew that he had a white blackbird in the grounds.

'Oh yes, we have some of those every year. Sometimes they have white speckles, or a white collar. Often they have white heads. We're hoping that this year we may get an all-white bird. We had a brood of white sparrows once; but of course these things don't breed true. They are sports.'

Agreed, I suppose; but I like to pretend that I think the blackbird, as well as all those sparrows, may have gone white with grief for the horrors of history. Why should they not embody the haunting spirits of forgotten prisoners who died alone in the dark, longing to be free as little birds?

No Apology

As one who likes to write about nature, I feel I ought to be ashamed of my ignorance of this vast subject; but why waste energy blushing when very little can be done about it? Subtraction of ignorance by addition of knowledge cannot diminish ignorance of an infinite subject. And sometimes I feel, a little complacently, that ignorance may be an asset, as it enables me to be astonished by commonplace things, and if I were not astonished, or moved in some way, then I wouldn't write. I wouldn't put pen to paper for a mere matter of fact. It also allows me a sense of progression — I feel that I learn something new each time I am surprised, which is often.

Furthermore, the knowing of names and the use of words can be, in some cases, a protection from direct experience. If I see a flower and don't know its name, it is impossible just to mutter 'coltsfoot, troublesome weed', and pass on. I really have to look at it. It is a stranger hailing me from the laneside. 'What is this?' I ask, and cannot answer. Then I ask 'What is it like?' and begin to take note. Leafless, as yet, fleshy stemmed; hairy golden face, like an early attempt at a dandelion. It is a childish drawing of the rayed sun by the earth.

If I see a dipper and do not know its name, I cannot just say 'dipper', and give it no more thought. 'What is that flash of white?' I wonder; 'Is it snow? Is it a scrap of foam, or a bit of paper bobbing about in the beck?' Then I see it is a small bird, somewhat larger than a sparrow, and beck-water brown all over but for a neat foam-white bib. It is a hardy Pennine bird, to be seen all winter, like the robin, but, unlike the robin it is very shy and comes nowhere near houses, though it can tolerate bridges very well. It haunts becks. Its white breast shines out from the peat-brown water and the rich green mosses as it perches on mid-stream stones, turning about and curtseying all the while, as though it has springs in its legs. It flies up and down stream, as though the river were its highway — which it is — and fishing-ground and pantry, too. Then it vanishes into a cave, or under a waterfall or an overhanging bank. So I go home and look it up. Thus I learn.

Ten years ago I scarcely knew an ash tree when I saw one. I didn't know the beckoning curve of their twigs, their vertically ridged bark, their black, hoof-like buds. I didn't know that sycamore trees had scaly bark like large cornflakes, or that beeches have a smooth skin (sometimes wrinkled about the joints like loose tights), and ideal for the carving of initials, apparently. After years in London, where I hardly knew what time of year it was, I had practically forgotten the names of the common flowers I had known as a child. Now, after years of haphazard study in the university of Horton-in-Ribblesdale, I am glad to have put the unseeing person that I was behind me; for the drawback of a too extreme ignorance is that what one doesn't know about tends to remain invisible. A bird is a mere bird, if it is anything at all, unless it is a kestrel or a bluetit, or something equally distinct and definite. Certain inconspicuous orchids might just as well be grass for the non-perceptive.

At one time I wouldn't have seen that tree-full of thrushes-with-a-difference, perching together eating the fruits of the hawthorn tree by the vicarage in cold weather. It would have been quite beyond me to suspect that they were fieldfares. I might not have noticed even those dramatically obvious, wide round-ended, slow-flapping-winged herons, with tucked-back heads and trailing legs, whose flight-path from the Ribble to destination as yet unknown (by me) has passed over our croft more or less daily throughout this winter. I wouldn't have noticed the returned lapwings flocking with gulls in mid-February. I might not have heard the first skylark singing over our croft on the 20th February. I must have noticed the wakened tortoiseshell butterfly fluttering against our windows, struggling to get out into the sunlight, for such have been familiar from childhood. I let it out, so it danced drunkenly away into what seemed like spring.

I think I might have recognised my first coltsfoot of the season, peering up between the flags of a deserted cottage, but, for certain, those enormous cordate leaves that grow on frequently-flooded stony ground beside the Ribble at midsummer were still 'wild rhubarb' to me, and not the late leaves of the fair coltsfoot's tender-eyed cousin — butterbur. So I wouldn't have noticed that these unspectacular pink flowers of early spring are already showing above ground, albeit swathed in protective bracts within which the separate flowers are packed together in one egg-shaped lump, something like a pineapple. They are greeted, of course, by a cold wind, a cloudy sky and a flurry of snow.

Dawns

After this half-term holiday our children will be going to school by daylight — no longer slinking along, semi-visible, close to the laneside walls in the dark. No more phosphorescent armbands or waistcoats will be necessary, and in only a few short weeks the sun will have been shining and the birds shouting for hours and hours while we have been asleep. This advantage carries with it its accompanying loss, as all advantages do, for we shall see no more compulsory dawns; and though dawn is a daily miracle, most of us miss it if we can.

Since Christmas, the first certain knowledge of morning has been conveyed to us by the row of lighted windows in the byre across the field, a sign that our neighbours were up and milking. Then, when our own lights were on, the sky beyond our window-panes faded from inky blue to paler and paler periwinkle violet, with snowdrifts shining luminous blue on the dark earth. After the children had set off into the unknown world of the dark, often in rain or snow, to catch their eight o' clock bus, and we had turned out our lights, we could see the horizon grow more and more distinct while our cock crew as though he took personal responsibility for the raising of the sun.

Mysterious grey distances outside came alive with anonymous birds making grating and grasshopperish noises. Rooks shouted hoarsely and wheeled about near their rookery. Berries of rain shone on bare twigs. A starling did an impersonation of a curlew, a contralto blackbird sang a short solo, and the morning air grew busier and busier with bird-traffic while the morning star disguised itself in the gradual crescendo of light before sunrise. At last a dazzling rim appeared over the south-west horizon and floodlit the peaks of Ingleborough and Whernside. When there was snow they shone like great white whales floating on a receding tide of shadow, cast by the shoulder of Pen-y-Ghent.

Because of these term-time glimpses, before I too set off for work, I thought it would be worthwhile to endure the dream-destroying shock of an alarm-clock in order to see the dawn voluntarily before it becomes too early to be feasible. Already, by getting up at seven-thirty on the first Saturday of the holiday, I was out only just in time.

It was quite light at eight, and perching birds were silhouetted amid the upper branches of the ash trees, as though they hoped to have a grandstand view of the sunrise. But the sky was uniformly overcast, and the sun rose invisibly, though its light, filtered through cloud, restored the colour to fields and rich green mosses on walls.

In a hilltop field I noticed a dotted line of about twelve new molehills, linked by ridges where the mole had burrowed close to the surface and stretched the turf into an arch. With an inquisitive finger I poked some ventilation holes into the damp earth to confirm that the underground really ran this way, and broke through into hollow darkness. The earth-heaps made earliest had been washed smooth by rain, but the most recent were still loose and crumbly. It would probably not have been difficult to locate the velvet engineer himself, but I felt that after what must have been a hard night's work, he deserved to fall asleep in peace, lullabied by the twittering of the birds prospecting for nest-sites — the first stutterings of spring's full chorus.

The National Anthem of the Robin

My bagpipe whistles WAR!
My flag of blood
Proclaims me master here
In this back-yard
Which is my native land;
You have been warned:
I fence my feeding-ground
With staves of sound.

Brave Robin stands alone;
Ice drips away.
When Wintertime is done
The Weddingday
Arrives. Keep out! Keep out!
It's matingtime.
For gentleness we shout
And mean no crime.

This selfishness is virtue;
We claim our rights
But have no wish to hurt you;
We seek no fights
And keep our boundaries
Without a gun,
For firing roundelays
Can murder none.

Hark, Hark!

About a year ago I had a discussion with a friend about which came first, larksong or snowdrops; so this year I took careful note, and it was on the 28th February that I first saw and heard a skylark soaring and singing while snowdrops were already hanging their white heads, like droplets of opaque ice, but they had not yet fully opened their three-bladed propeller of petals. Before that date I had heard snatches of song and caught glimpses of grounded skylarks perched on walls or running about and feeding in the fields.

I once believed, mistakenly, that larks fed on airborne insects as they sang high over the fields, but their music is a territorial song, a kind of national anthem, that lays claim to the acre or so of grassland below their upward spiralling and windborne circling. In spite of this, fortunately, no farmer ever arms himself to defend his land from invading skylarks.

Clearly the larks like to make sure of nesting-room early in the season, and on the 1st March several were up and chortling away in the rain. I was curious, during those wild days when March was coming in like a lion, to see if, and how, these tiny birds could keep up their singing in the force-nine gales that were blowing from the east. Surely they would climb the air to claim a field by Douk Ghyll, and descend, if they could descend at all, to find themselves the confused owners of a bald patch of limestone on Moughton, a field in Crummackdale, or even in Clapham. So I went out to look, and actually saw a desperate skylark climbing up the invisible wind by means of a most astonishing aeronautical skill — tacking from side to side and somehow using the giant forces against him for his own purposes — and he stayed up, making his musical announcements, for a surprisingly long time before he dropped to earth in a lull of the wind. He then scurried about to find food to replace the large quantity of calories such a performance must have burnt up.

Further up the hill I saw a small group of larks, disinclined to argue about territories, crouching together on the ground, having no wish to be blown adrift in the wild current of the air, and they only reluctantly let go of the ground when I approached.

As the lion of March grew tamer, the larks rose up from all over the dale like tiny bubbles in water that is just beginning to boil. They made me think of Edward and Laura, the children in Flora Thompson's *Lark Rise*, who, in a long-forgotten spring towards the end of the last century, leapt up and down on the awakening fields shouting out 'We're bubbles of earth, we're bubbles of earth!'

Larks are just like bubbles of earth, dancing away, shrilling and trilling, in sunshine, drizzle, or unseen, among the squeaks of lapwings and the operatic arias of curlews, in mists.

Lapwings and curlews stop up very late at night, and sing in the dark, while the lark goes to bed with the sun, but he has a well-earned reputation for early rising. Yet, early though he rises, when the clocks were put forward this year it became necessary, for a week or so, to get up before him. Then he started to sing with the alarm clock, when the window was grey. By the time I could be up, dressed, and outside to listen, rooks, wood-pigeons, curlews, blackbirds, thrushes, chaffinches and wrens were singing too; and, blown about on gusts and gales of passion, like the lovers in the second circle of Dante's *Inferno*, groups of two or three birds dashed about, recklessly fast, in early morning love-chases. But the skylark was spiralling up and up, towards the shining vapour-trail of a jet which, far above the earth, caught the light of the yet unrisen sun. She rose to where she could see the valley, with its walled fields hanging like a hammock below, with March hares racing, weightless as shadows, up the steep hillsides, and the grey earth rolling over in her sleep towards the sunrise.

Buds

The darkest part of the night comes just before dawn, so they say, but it is the whitest part of the winter that comes before spring; and because 'while drifts still lie along the wallsides more snow must come to fetch them away', the hills have been turning white, then green, then white again then green again, several times in these last few weeks. This process might go on indefinitely, as the snow that comes to fetch away the drifts must, in its turn, lie as white stripes along the northern sides of walls until yet more snow comes to fetch it away, too: but each time it reappears the green is greener, and the white, when it returns, is more transparent, and the lying snow retreats further up the hillsides.

While the alternate blanching and greening of the landscape has been going on, the returned lapwings and curlews have been crying over the snow-patched fields and preparing to set up house. At evening the March hares have been running about on Whitber, fox-red in the sunset light, with the same idea in their disturbed minds. Thawed snow from the fells comes roaring out of the hillsides as becks in flood, and the March winds roar in the trees wherein strong rivers of sap are rising without a sound. This silent flood is visible as a new and increasingly intense colour hovering about groups of trees. A haze of purple clothes the branches of wakening copses. This is not a trick of the light, or of aerial perspective — the twigs and buds of many trees really are purplish-crimson coloured in spring.

We suffer from colour-prejudices concerning trees. We think that trunks are brown and leaves, as a rule, are green. This idea of brown tree-trunks originates, I think, in childhood. Tree-trunks are made of wood and so are tables and chairs. Tables and chairs are brown and so, children appear to reason, are tree-trunks. As children we scrub away at all the various brown tablets in the paintbox in order to give that dark-oak or gingery-varnish hue to the drainpipe tree-trunks of our forests. Then one day we open our eyes, and we see that tree-trunks are grey or silver, greenish or mottled blue with lichen. In autumn I have seen hawthorn trunks and branches bright green with small mosses, and loaded with crimson berries; now they are still green with the same mosses, but they have crimson twigs, blood-red thorns, and pink buds breaking along the twigs.

Elms are already in flower, with red cone-like roses, not much bigger than buds, adding their mites of colour to the purple haze about the trees. Snaky horse-chestnut twigs are terminated by bulging brown clubs which exude the sticky sweat of spring. The blunt buds spaced along larch twigs are loosening and turning pale at their tips. Sycamore buds glimmer like light green candle flames. They do not contribute to the general purpleness, and nor does the wary grey-twigged ash, which knows better than to loosen its hoof-like black buds much before midsummer. But while the ashes carry the winter well into May, many beeches and oaks still wear a rustling underskirt of last year's dead leaves, thus carrying autumn through winter into spring. But, in spite of these burdens, there can be no doubt about it — the great majority of buds at present declare for spring.

The Shepherd

One morning a week or so ago I heard a whistle outside and looked out of the door to see who was coming, but saw no-one. Then I heard the whistle again, but louder and nearer, and saw that it was not a human sound at all but the first curlew coming back to the moors, cutting through the wind and calling piercingly: it was the vanguard of the spring. As I took the children across the fields to school, a lark flew up, performing its musical rope-trick, climbing note over note up an invisible thread of song. It scattered notes over the tawny fields that resembled blankets pressed flat under the recently withdrawn ice. The nearly vertical hillsides were still patterned by dwindling snowdrifts that appeared like patches of grey-white sky seen through holes gouged out of the cardboard cut-out fells.

Each day the pattern of drifts on the fell becomes more sparsely scattered, the brown grass grows an eye of green in it, and the birds who have come through begin to sing victoriously, and grow excited about nesting. Pieces of straw, a long piece of white string, and tufts of wool, go undulating through the air, towed home by nest-proud birds. As the children ride their tricycles along the lanes ahead of me, it appears that a great queen has been walking about and flinging golden coins on either side of her path. The two greedy beggars, my children, snatch up this largesse eagerly, the scattered discs of gold proving to be the whiskery faces of coltsfoot, and the shiny, clean-shaven ones, of celandine.

And now a shriller note is heard among the deep belching of the ewes in the fields, and small white drifts of snow lying up under the walls prove to be the first lambs, newly born and sleeping off this staggering experience.

'How is the lambing going?' I ask our neighbour, a farmer.

'It's not started so badly, considering. We've got five pair of twins already.' He beckoned me over. 'Come and feel the weight of this lamb. It's just born and it feels as heavy as many at three week old. I should think he weighs fifteen pound.'

I obediently lifted the long-legged, weak-kneed lamb. Its birth-bedraggled coat was still in tight wet curls that would fluff out as they dried. It felt rather slimy, and its umbilicus dangled bloodily.

'His mother had a big lamb last year', said the farmer, 'but this year I thought it were going to be twins.'

'Do you really know all your sheep separately, one from the other?' I asked.

'Aye. I've been working with them all my life, d' you see. If one of them's lambed out on the fells, and my son comes and tells me of it, he can always make me understand which one it is.'

'But you have hundreds.'

'Aye.'

'How do you describe them? Where do you begin?'

'Oh, there's always summat about them, or summat's happened to them, like.'

'They all look the same to me', I said townily, 'how can anyone tell them apart?'

'It's living with them, d' you see', the shepherd said patiently, 'all your life. You get to know them.'

It pleased me to think that every anonymous grey smudge nibbling the grass on the fellside was known as an individual to its owner; and I wished that I could believe that every inconspicuous grey woman had a good shepherd of this order. The welfare state does not fill this role.

The shepherd became very technical about sheep-breeding, and his discourse was mainly above my head. It concerned Wensleydales and Dalesbred, Whitefaced Sheep and Cheviots, and as he rambled on I considered that we had first come to this Yorkshire dale when my elder son, now scrambling up and down a steep and stony field with his younger brother, was only six weeks old. It was late April and the air was full of the crying of lambs. I sometimes used to think that the lambs' voices were the baby's bleating complaint of a voice, and I ran to see what ailed him when he was quite content.

Often, as I sat beside the window feeding him in the grey light of dawn, I watched the pale grey lambs playing in the field outside. Those lambs, which looked to me, but not to their shepherd, exactly like this year's lambs, grew to be sheep in one summer, and have long since become dowdy matrons, or mutton, or patriarchal rams, the fathers of flocks. But my son is only now at the lamb-like stage, and at least another six years of lambhood stretch before him. Indeed, 'it is not easily the clay grows tall' and a human being is made. And yet we squander these slowly built human lives so recklessly, by the thousand, as though they were no more than numbers: perhaps we should never have learned to count.

My son acquired, on his recent birthday, a model *Bismarck*-building set, and it stated calmly on the packet, as a matter of unemotional interest, that when the *Bismarck* went down there were only 115 survivors out of a crew of 2,000. And we, at the time, rejoiced. And the sinking of the *Bismarck* was only very primitive and old-fashioned mass-destruction. We can do much better now, so we may rejoice a thousandfold.

Then I remembered that a sheep belonging to our neighbour the farmer had once fallen into a dry well on our croft, and lay there at the bottom, mute and uncomplaining, after the manner of sheep. And when this big man with even bigger boots, and the heavy unhurried gait of one who walks about all day, and old clothes smelling of dung, and his tongue perpetually damning and blasting the weather which can never please him, came and lifted the sheep from the well and laid it on the grass, in the knowledge that its back was broken and it would die, his face worked and he wept. And although they say of him locally that he is one who would 'halve currants', it was not for the five or six pounds that a sheep was worth that he wept, but for an individual sheep that was dying.

I cannot help wishing that I believed that we, too, have a good shepherd that cares for us in this way, and not that we are, collectively, supposed to be our own good shepherd: for we are not reliable.

In Praise of Also-Rans

Every year at about this time, when leggy lambs are staggering in the fields, celandine is opening underfoot and larks are larking about overhead, and the weather is liable to provide anything from serenest sunshine to snow, the long-distance runners gather in Chapel-le-Dale for the annual Three Peaks race.

This year, on the day before, a north-easter had been blowing, and the peaks, when the clouds allowed them to be visible, were silver with snow. In the valley it was raining gustily. But on the Sunday of the race, though the cold wind still blew, there was fitful sunshine as well as fitful rain and hail, and the peaks were striped black and white with thaw. They looked slippery and dangerous from a distance, but nevertheless nearly 200 heroic runners from all over Britain, clad in absurd little shorts, set off from the Hill Inn in Chapel-le-Dale at eleven o'clock.

They were not due to run through Horton-in-Ribblesdale till at least half an hour later, but the village car-park was already overflowing with cars, the lanes were full of friends and supporters of runners, and almost the entire population of the village had turned out, as usual. The pub on the route was a hive of holiday activity.

The first runners appeared as tiny pale specks filtering down from Moughton to move over the Beecroft fields, looking, from the other side of the valley, like stray marbles rolling gently down a slightly inclined surface. They disappeared as they funnelled through the gate to the level crossing over the railway, and then ran the quarter mile of level road to the Crown Inn, where they took to the bushes and trees along Brantsghyll's course.

Scores of runners, singly and in groups, were scrambling their way along Brantsghyll beck when I set off up the lane to the point where the racers' track crosses the Pennine Way. By the time I had huffed and puffed my way there, the leaders had been and gone, and were over the hills and away. A group of upright figures, like a cluster of whiskers, was just visible on Pen-y-Ghent's dark crest. Across Horton Scar the human marbles were rolling uphill now, on their second peak of the morning, powered by the gravity-defying human will. Only stragglers were still crossing the lane. One — wearing thick lenses and a knee-bandage — limped gamely through the gate. The next had a lighter and springier step than many of his forerunners. 'You're late', said someone's tactless child, but the runner skipped on, regardless.

'He must know that he has no chance of winning now', I thought, 'but he keeps on, and this is fine.' There can be only one winner, but no race without the others who must run, after a while, for the sake of running, for a curious kind of joy and self-conquest: to overcome again and again the impulse to slow down, stop, lie down, rest and roll down hill. So they pit legs, lungs and hearts against the everlastingly upstairs gradients of the peaks, which are almost as exhausting on the way down.

I know, for I myself have done the Three Peaks; but I have done them one at a time, in the same way as I knocked off my O and A levels, and I have always taken every opportunity to stop and watch plovers, ring ouzels and dippers; to pick flowers, collect fossils, and admire the view. I take sandwiches, tea-flasks, drawing materials, children and dogs; and the expedition lasts all day. But these runners, even the losers, do all three peaks in three or four hours. Already, as the last cotton-shirted, flimsy-shorted runner plodded, almost walking, up the long straight wallside that leads to the top of Pen-y-Ghent, tiny figures were visible running along the dark horizon of undulating moorland which forms the second side of the Three Peaks twenty-five mile triangle, and leads to the third and highest peak.

Whernside, to the north, was now veiled by swiftly moving curtains of rain and hail, and gusts of spray were already wetting us as we stood on the Pennine Way, talking of lambing and of walls broken by hikers now, so I went on my way downhill, home again, not knowing the name of this year's winner, and not caring overmuch, but thinking 'All honour to the also-rans'.

Moorland Study (1960)

An April Morning

We had become accustomed to submarine living on soil that, like an animal body, was about seventy-five per cent water, and in an atmosphere that soaked us through in a few minutes even when it wasn't actually raining. We had adapted ourselves.

It had begun to seem preferable to live on an earth swathed in a grey cloud canopy, and to be burrowing about in water vapour over squelchy ground that glittered with surface water. The becks were almost continuously in spate, and from all the waterfalls came a hissing and rumbling sound, as of motorway traffic. Only occasionally a ray of sunlight broke through the cloud roof to illuminate a lucky distant hill, and it seemed cosier and softer to be thus protected from infinite space and the terrifying numberlessness of the stars — until last Saturday.

Then we woke to a dazzling morning. The sky was an intense violet-blue all over, except for the heads and shoulders of a few white cumulus ghosts that waited patiently at the edges of the great round table of the world. So the sun shone, and aconites and crocuses opened to catch the light in their coloured cups. Overhead was an endless depth of blueness, and, like a tiny silver clapper in an infinite bell, the skylark was singing.

As I was fetching our milk up the lane, two birds dashed across the track only a yard or two in front of me. They alighted on the laneside wall. They were so preoccupied with their own emotions that they did not notice me.

They were skylarks, perching a few feet from each other with crests erect, tails tilted up at an angle of forty-five degrees, and wings held a little way off from their sides. They flicked their tails and curtseyed to each other — each with eyes only for the other bird, and none for me. I stood perfectly still. Was this a courtship or a confrontation, love or politics, a wedding or an election? I suspected that the birds were both male, but wasn't sure.

The formal bowing and curtseying continued, accompanied by a vocal argument. It was not the usual lark-song aria, but a less melodious recitative. Then the birds rose up off the wall, hovering a few feet above it and still arguing. They appeared to have become buoyant with passion. They met, bumped and grappled in mid-air. One flew off to alight on the field. The other followed it. The musical argument and the formal bowing and curtseying began again. Once more they rose up off their hard-edged navy-blue shadows and hovered a few feet above them, vociferating. I heard their bodies collide in the air, and there was another flutter of four wings enclosing an airborne battle.

Another bird arrived, and then another. These seemed to be only spectators. Now I could assume that the two arguing birds were male and the quieter, waiting birds, female. The formal bowing was resumed. The birds rose up and collided in mid-air once more, then one made off, followed by one of the females. Meanwhile the other female was flattening herself on the ground, and as soon as the other male had gone, the victor of these not-very-serious battles alighted beside her and without any ceremony — such as one might expect, of bowing, curtseying, or singing and dancing — mated with her.

Meanwhile the defeated bird — or perhaps it was yet another — had climbed the air and was singing joyfully overhead.

Today it is still singing, though the canopy of water vapour and the grey drizzle, which seem to compose our natural habitat, have returned.

Haze in the Dale (1961)

Magpies

One's for sorrow; two appear for joy
to glitter along the edge of a threadbare wood
and overlook the scavenging riffraff rooks
and sober, industrious jackdaws that walk the field
prodding the mud for food.

More like enormous tropical butterflies
than British birds, they are crows that have won the pools
and wear evening dress all day, so, with springy strut,
they show off satin shirts, white epaulettes,
and iridescent, green and blue silk tails.

With flashy wings they flutter, freewheel, flap,
seem casual, but loiter with intent;
through spyholes in black hoods they case the joint —
this green upholstered landscape — preen and scratch
and wait for singing chickens' eggs to hatch.

Fine feathers make fine crows — mere liar birds —
both lucky and unlucky, like the rest.
Perhaps some gamekeeper could not resist
the target of those guiltless villains' vests;
or have they flown to roost in taller trees

with better views, and built a bonfire nest
such as success deserves? For I have missed
my first and second murderers for days:
now hear them shake their bones, deep in the woods,
haunting, immortal in their shot-silk shrouds.

A Sun King with Earth Queens

The metallic cough of the coppery King-in-exile
heralds the pheasants' arrival, requests our attention
although he has nothing to say but 'Look at me, look
at the burnished scales of my soft, ceremonial armour,
the springy plumes of my cantilevered tail
and gold-buttoned armistice poppies on either cheek;
observe my priestly collar and sea-green cowl
but do not notice my modestly camouflaged Queens.'

During our absence, one morning, he dropped us a feather;
its chestnut filaments had been dipped in sunlight
though, near its root, it was grey with thermal down.
This gold-tipped message informed us that he had called.
Twice daily he ushers his shy harem through our weeds;
his seven furtive princesses in brown-speckled tweeds
consider that ours is a safe house. Increasingly silent,
we bang few doors and fail to mow our lawns.

Perched on the topmost rail of our shaky fence,
the resplendent King proclaims a palace-garden
of coltsfoot beds, and hedges spread into thickets;
his dowdy Queens nod automatic approval,
pecking at mosses between wild raspberry canes.
If I go out with the washing, I beg their pardon,
conceding squatters' rights to the Wilderness,
and title deeds to the Royal Concubines.

Dappled with sunspots, deep in the undergrowth,
they crouch, disguised as shadows or drifts of leaves,
and brood over crucibles full of the Royal Genes.
The gilded King steps out and coughs, midfield,
to draw the fire of our attention: 'Look
at my eldorado armour, my glaring eyes
buttoning blood-petalled poppies for brothers you killed;
my Queens are restoring the dead in their time-machines.'

Melodrama by Sunlight

Surely it could not be I that caused the alarmed commotion among the birds, for I had been sitting quite still for at least an hour, drawing the coltsfoot flowers. I was pursuing my absurd ambition to record the changing constellations of common weeds that appear on the ground through spring and summer, and this was the coltsfoot season. Near to the lemon-yellow whiskery discs of the coltsfoot, a fragment of pale blue starling's egg gleamed on the dark moss, and in and, out of crevices in the overhanging crag that all but enclosed this haunted place, starlings went to and fro feeding nestlings. A wren sang from a little way down the beck, and blackbirds were going about their April business. Then, suddenly, a wood-pigeon clapped away out of a high beech and set up this great commotion of alarm notes. The wren started an indignant tut-tut-tutting, scolding and swearing, and the blackbirds shrilled their warning Morse, accentuating it by a flicking of tails and twitching of wings. The dipper was bobbing up and down in anxiety on a rock near the entrance of its cave. Something was obviously up. Was another human approaching? I hoped not: but there was a human-like whistle from the edge of the trees. Perhaps it was not quite human enough. Then there was a *kee-wit, kee-wit* sound from the dark crack beneath the deeply undercut top layer of the crag.

The birds became noisier and more excited. There was a low, clarinet-like call from the furthest trees, answered by a fussy, petulant sound from the crag. The trembling clarinet-call sounded louder, nearer; hollow and eerie: and a great, moth-silent, greyish bird flew out from the shadows of a dark shelf high in the crag, formed where the limestone bedding plane had sagged away from the layers on top.

The owl's flight curved upward, and the bird perched on a horizontal branch of a dead ash quite close to me. It was very large; a Goliath to the wrens and blackbirds.

From a dark horse-chestnut tree, sprigged with unfolding leaves, the clarinet-like call came again. The owl in the tree answered — *kik-kik-kik.*

The David-sized birds flew, aggressively shrieking, towards the tree whence the voice seemed to issue, but it sounded again — louder — nearer — thrilling and trembling. The small birds shouted their ineffectual alarm, as the incoming owl, with one more undulating hoot, now arrived on perfectly silent wings, and, wasting no more breath or time in announcements or conversation, the owls met with a great flapping and flutter of wings on the sunlit ash tree branch. Were they kissing? Mating? Or was one feeding the other? The sun shone in my eyes. It was difficult to distinguish exactly what was happening until they sat quietly, side by side, blinking, for a few moments: then the incoming one flew silently away, back to the chestnut tree. My eye followed his flight and marked where he settled to look like the blunt-ended stump of a branch, but when I looked back to the ash tree where the owls had met, the first one had silently vanished.

The small birds resumed their business. Blackbirds sang and starlings continued shuttling to and from the crag with edible beakfuls, but my coltsfoot felt the evening's approach and was shutting up shop. A pale half-moon already gleamed in the sky. So, causing all the usual human disturbance, I crashed my way out of a nature that had absorbed me.

Micro-Climates

The climate at Clapham or Austwick is milder than that of Horton-in-Ribblesdale. Even in Settle the spring starts earlier and progresses faster than it does here. Now I have found that even by travelling more than 300 miles north, to the Outer Hebrides, the descent from our 900 feet to sea-level, plus the influence of the Atlantic drift, equalises the prevailing temperature, or even tilts the balance slightly in favour of those remote northern islands. Certainly, the west coast of mainland Scotland is positively tropical compared with Horton. There, larches were vividly green as we passed by two weeks ago. The gorse was in full golden flower, and the broom was beginning.

I used to think that our sub-arctic conditions here were a micro-climate, but having been reading, on our only cold wet day on Harris, a book on the natural history of the Highlands and Islands, I discovered how small a micro-climate can really be. For instance, the lee side of a tree or a stone can shelter a micro-climate; a southward tilt of the ground, or south face a north face of a wall create micro-climates; and the upper branches of trees live and move in different micro-climates from the lower branches. I found myself observing micro-climates everywhere. On Harris we picnicked on the north-east side of a boulder which was shaggy with green lichen. The other side was scrubbed bare by those Atlantic gales which have 3,000 miles of ocean across which they can pick up speed.

Stopping for a while on our homeward journey, we wandered among the dark conifers of a forestry plantation. A high wind was blowing over the loch on the other side of the road, but among the trees the air was still and warm, while high above the perpetual shade of the forest floor — where wood-sorrel and mosses proliferated — the treetops were threshing and hissing like sea-waves.

Since we have been back home I have been peering into those micro-jungles sheltered by the deep grykes in local limestone-pavement country. At Southerscales, by Ingleborough, the surface of the ground looks like a desert — a desert in which a sparse scattering of stunted ashes, hazels and sycamores seems to be sinking into white stone. A closer look shows that most of these trees are rooted five or six feet down, and have been able to make a start in life only because the grykes already contained some soil where mosses, grasses, ferns and less ambitious plants were growing. Some of the deeper and more terrifying cracks in this ideal leg-breaking terrain contain deserts like the surface of pavements. Perhaps they may hold a few sheeps' bones, or the sound of subterranean water, but too little sun penetrates far enough for anything green to grow. In others, hartstongue ferns hang, overlapping as though to drink from a well, and there are whorls of maiden-hair, debris of dead bracken, and pale green shepherds' crooks of uncoiling ferns, several feet down, in the shade.

In shallower, more basin-like grykes, glossy bluebell leaves, dog's mercury, wood-sorrel and other woodland plants grow succulent and green. Wild strawberry, lily-of-the-valley and lords-and-ladies' leaves deny eloquently that we are on the moon-desert that appears at a superficial glance. In each individual gryke, we are, in fact, in a micro-climate. In this one place they all have much in common, but each deep, self-contained little world also differs from the others according to its depth, width and water supply. From some grykes peer clumps of large yellow primroses, in full, non-wind-battered flower; but others, and, to me, the most beautiful just now, contain the pale wood-anemones, their delicate leaves tinged with purple, their petals waxen-white. And in a few weeks there will be *Primula farinosa*, and globe-flowers in the more open spaces. But there is no need to anticipate.

An Easter Egg

The hen, who had long been in that inward-looking state of indifference to time which cannot be called 'patience', because while it lasts the bird is unaware of waiting for anything but is simply possessed by a clutch of possibilities, like a poet at work, was at last driven off her nest by a wind-driven hailstorm. She had sat and brooded long enough for seven of her ten eggs to have hatched, so their fluff-covered contents followed her. The three remaining eggs were abandoned: pale tombs of unfulfilled potentiality. They were as cold as pebbles when I found them and picked them up to bring them indoors, wondering what to do with them. I thought they might be interesting for the boys to dissect, for they probably contained fully-formed birds. One of them had even got as far as beginning to crack. It bore a little hole, with radiating hairlines, as though someone had thrown a small stone from the inside. The tip of a beak was just visible.

With a passing regret for the wastefulness of nature, I left them on the draining-board in the kitchen and temporarily forgot them. Half an hour later, passing by, it appeared to me that the tiny beak-tip moved. Had it given a gasp? I picked the egg up and looked at it closely. It was still as cold as marble but, after all, the kitchen was a good deal warmer than the wild weather outside. Coldness is relative. Perhaps it had a spark of life left in it, and perhaps the warm kitchen was reviving it.

Holding the living pebble, I breathed gently into the tiny hole. The beak responded by gasping again, and moving unmistakably. I breathed more warm air into it: the kiss of life for an egg. The beak gasped again.

Hastily I boiled a kettle and filled a hot-water bottle. I put the egg into one of the children's woollen hats, placed it on the hot-water bottle and left it.

But I couldn't leave it for long. I kept returning and peeping, and turning the egg over to be warmed equally on all sides. Within an hour the beak was uttering tiny squeaks; the egg was chirping, and, little by little, the hole was chipped larger.

All day I was obsessed by this egg. The beak moved restlessly and the hole opened sideways, jaggedly, round the biggest diameter. Flakes of eggshell cracked away. The egg was unzipping itself: but so slowly.

I knew I must keep my hands off. An egg must not be helped. To struggle out on its own is a part of a chicken's development. A Caesarean delivery, in the case of chicks, produces a weakling. One must be indifferent to be kind.

We must all fight our own battles, but the chick's battle lasted all day. When the children came in from school, the egg was bleeping vigorously and the crack was nearly meeting itself. There were glimpses of hair through the torn membrane, and a scaly claw gripped the edge of the crack. A shining slit broke a bruise-blue bulge that must be an eye. It all looked very sinister and not at all lovable. It might, after all, be anything that we were letting loose on the world: a poisonous reptile, a dragon, a hairy hybrid that would grow and grow, devouring other chickens, uprooting plants and trees, gulping down people.

This mere egg was obviously looming too large in my mind. I tried to concentrate on tea while the bleeping continued and the struggle to be born intensified.

The children and I watched, fascinated, while milk over-boiled and toast burned. The kitchen filled with smoke as our little dragon heaved and strained, raising its hinged lid. We opened the door to let out the smoke, and turned off the stove. The creature gave another heave. Then again. The membrane tore completely and the lid fell away. A wet and hairy head lolled out. The mini-monster, whatever it was, rested for a few moments and then gave another convulsive push, exerting its whole body, inflating all its muscles, uncurling its spine, and using its inexperienced legs as levers, so it fell out of its egg onto the woollen hat.

It was a chick alright: an exhausted, wet-haired, pink-skinned chick, as weak as a newborn baby. It lay on its bed, unable to lift its head, like a swimmer thrown up on the beach of life after many days in the sea. Its fluff was wet and looked like shredded string. Its half-closed eyes appeared to have been blacked at some point in the fight to arrive. It was not at all cuddly, nor in the least like an Easter card. But it was triumphant. Though it sat with its legs re-folded underneath it, it was manifestly impossible that it could be repacked into the halved eggshell. It was in the world.

We refilled the hot-water bottle, put the chick back inside the hat, threw the eggshell into the compost bucket and resumed the preparation of tea.

We ate tea and we washed up; then we looked at the bird. It had dried out and fluffed up, and its eyes were wide open. It lay there comfortably, folded up to resemble a toy duck, raising its head and looking about it.

As the east wind was still blowing outside, and intermittent hailstorms rattled down on our roof, we decided to bring the mother hen and all the other chicks in for the night. We put them in a cardboard box with straw, pellets, millet seed and water, and when the mother was settled and feeling at home, we put the new chick with its brothers and sisters beneath her until morning. After another day on the hot-water bottle, with millet seed, and another night with brothers and sisters, indoors, we put the Lazarus chick out into the innocently calm and sunny weather of its third day of life, with that living substitute for a hot-water bottle, its mother, so that now the whole lot — the hen like a white ship surrounded by tugs — is voyaging over and through the greening sea of grass that is our acre, and soon we will be unable to tell which one it was we rescued.

Newly-Hatched Nestling

Blind robot-face,
small alien
with hot, pink, waxy skin
and dragon fingertoes:
gutbag with legs,
mildewed with tufts of down,
you stretch your feeble neck
and wave about
hunger's two-petalled flower—
your gaping beak.
Your swollen, bruise-blue eyes,
your feather boa,
are horrible, and yet
what love you inspire.

Chickens

The law of 'to those that have shall be given' seems to apply to those who have livestock as well as other things, such as money or education, for the three chrysanthemum-coloured bantam fowls we were given last autumn are now increased to fourteen.

Those first three, last September, settled down very quickly to a life of scratching up our garden and eating like wolves, for which we forgave them in the hope of eggs, though their sexes were as yet indeterminate; and because they made us all feel very superior by their obviously low IQs, though they all had sense enough for chickens.

In some ways they were very skilful. They would step delicately and cautiously out of their hutch in the morning, placing their scaly feet here and there with the deliberate control of dancers, to peck up corn with precision, and then to forage for themselves and find all sorts of edible seeds and grubs in the grass. They had a strong instinct for togetherness, and, when feeding in the long grass, one of them would, every now and then, extend its neck into a kind of watchtower to look round in all directions, and thus keep a round and mindless eye on the cat and the people. When they feared themselves threatened, they scattered out of reach into trees or onto walls, for these bantams could fly, unlike their heavyweight relations. We ourselves became so used to the scale of mini-chickens that if we met a normal hen in the lane it appeared to be a short-legged ostrich or an effeminate eagle.

Yet, though our light-weight hens may have been able to fly, they certainly couldn't think. One autumn night a gale blew the roof off the chicken-house, but when we went out in the morning — rather late, as it happened — they were still standing waiting to be let out of the door. This is typical chicken behaviour; they acquire a few useful habits and then behave rather like machines. Seeing that we had three orange-and-tawny fowls, our neighbour brought us a twin pair of white silkies, with topknots of white feathers which made them appear intellectual, though, if anything, they were less bright than the others. He also brought us a fiery, conker-red cock, with hairy, high-heeled feet, for it had become clear that all our birds were hens. So then the number of our fowls became potentially infinite.

They began to lay in February, and in March the prettiest hen went broody; so we marked, and let her keep, ten eggs. Then she sat and she sat, swelling ferociously and cackling hoarsely if anyone approached her treasure hoard.

The other hens got into the box beside her to lay their eggs where they, too, would be sat on, so we had to brave much pecking to retrieve them.

Once a day the devoted broody hen got up off her eggs for food, drink, and a little exercise. Then, all the time she was off, the cock, and the other hens, tried to chase her back to her duties. They even led her back, and, one by one, all the other hens went broody and sat with her in the box, so that it became a regular sit-in. No-one was laying eggs any more — just sitting and sitting, not even knitting.

We managed to cure all the excess aunts and would-be mothers of 'clocking' by shutting them up under a box for a few days, and, a week after Easter, the first egg hatched. So there lay on the hay among the warm and pulsating, but as yet impassive, eggs, a wet, surprised, exhausted and rather dark-haired chick, whose mother continued to treat it much as though it were still an egg for a day or two, while the other eggs hatched. First they showed cracks near the blunt end, then a beak from inside pecked a hole which, chip by chip, grew larger, and extended all the way round the egg until it met itself. Then, by dint of flexing its muscles and pushing hard, the incarcerated chick eventually broke the shell in two and tumbled out. So these magic chicken-seeds really worked, and were alive and well. Not only could we award our stupid chickens GCSEs in laying, but A levels in hatching as well.

The mother hen came out and about in the world again with eight bleeping puff-balls (one failed to hatch and one was a weakling so we nursed it on a hot water-bottle in a box indoors), and we found ourselves witnessing the education of chickens. After three weeks immolation, the hen took her family further and further from the nest-box every day, stopping often to give them all warm-ups, so that she became not only mother and teacher but house as well. Her wings drooped and became eaves, her under-plumage became upholstery; and the little ones disappeared, chirping like children, under her breast and tail, and into their feather-tiled house. Between these breaks she showed them how to peck and where to drink. She showed them how to scratch up the earth with their feet to find grubs, and how to take dust-baths. After a fortnight, two or three of the earliest hatched could take short flights, of a foot or so, comparable to the Wright brothers' first success; and they all had fairly well-developed wing feathers. They were losing their tabby-kittenish markings, and getting the slightly vulturish expressions of immature fowls.

They are on their way to their own first eggs and first-class degrees in chickendom.

The Bird Garden at Harewood

The lifers hunch on their perches
waiting for mealtimes, dreaming, remembering
broken promises overheard in the egg,
expectations printed in kidnapped genes
of embryos incubated under lamps
or hatched by fostering bantams in this garden.

Never quite warm enough, the Northern sunlight
shines obliquely, casting long cold shadows.
Peruvians and Amazonians,
a Balinese, and Indian Jungle Fowls —
whose vivid feathers reflect ancestral heat —
wait in their aviaries for life to start.

The great owls doze, but, through insomniac nights,
how can they soar? Seeing the stars through mesh
they imagine forests where they need not hunt,
being deprived of hunger. Through vague days
they yawn, and stretch unnecessary wings —
round-ended, downy feathered, lined for silence.

Two Demoiselles, in dresses out of Vogue,
wear quilly pompoms crowning skull-tight bonnets;
one Demoiselle, being male, opens his wings
to dance a courtship dance; he limps for love, lightly
on spring-hinged legs, because one wing
is pinioned, pruned for his own good.

Rendered flightless to keep them paradise-prisoned,
the crippled dancers pain us with their beauty.
The female spreads her asymmetrical shawl,
hops too high and falls like a hamstrung doll
of walking-sticks and feathers; when risen again
both puppets exit left, to their private limbo.

Ducks are a simpler matter. On the lake
the painted Mandarins move like happy toys;
and beauty makes excuses for the theft
of live components out of Nature's process
into this Bird Museum, these prison gardens
where long lives wither slowly as unspent fortunes.

A Moralist

The gamekeeper was standing outside the market-town grocery, waiting for his wife. He wore his usual timeless tweed suit with baggy knee breeches, in which he stalks the moors through winter and summer, for 'if it keeps t' cold out, stands to reason it 'll keep t' hot out as well'.

As usual he is not being serious, for he seldom allows himself to be. He is the local wit. One may meet him in the post office on a drenching morning when the rain has been siling down for days, and he will say, in a mincing accent: 'Remarkably heavy dew for the time of year, don't you think?' He and the fishing bailiff have a subversive song-and-dance routine that they perform in the pub at Christmas, and on bank holidays he has been known to announce that he's going out to shoot 'the bloody 'ikers'. But underneath the jokiness is a serious man, learned in his trade, who appreciates the mystery that is nature.

We had been exchanging pleasantries, dredging our minds for jokes about the weather, and torturing language into puns. I had reached the moment when I either moved on and continued shopping, which is what I ought to have been doing, or else we said a few more meaningful, and perhaps provocative, words.

'I've been doing something that will annoy you, I'm afraid', I said, and went on to tell him how we had sheltered and restored to health a member of Satan's black flock, an item of gamekeeper's bane, a black-hearted bird, a symbol of death and decomposition, a sign — contradicting the rainbow — that life and beauty cannot possibly win while this winged grave and living black-hole in the animate world, this carrion bird, this Crow still flourishes in our midst.

Some children had brought me a one-eyed and starving bird, which I had nursed back to health. He appeared to know already, and, from his scorn, I understood he had already discussed the matter. Villages are like that.

'If you'd left it alone it would be dead by now and t' world would be a better place. It will have to go through it all again.'

'It may be lucky', I said, 'and does it not have its place in keeping the balance of nature?'

'Nature's been unbalanced for centuries. We try to keep the balance that suits us.'

'Nevertheless, I see my place in the scheme of things as to be myself, and to obey my own instincts, not anyone else's. If my instincts tell me to cherish carrion crows, without calculation, but perhaps more out of interest and fascination than love, then I do so.'

'Nasty, wicked, filthy birds. What about when they kill whole nest-fulls of partridge chicks, just as they hatch? Would you love and cherish them then? What about the partridges? What about those poor parent birds?'

'Nature's cruel, I admit, but carrion crows have parental feeling too; and I can't be anything but neutral in this natural war.'

'Would you be so neutral when sheep's buried in t' snowdrift, and a carrion crow comes and picks out its eyes, leaving the sheep alive? Would you be so neutral then? Would you be neutral in t' spring, when a crow descends on a newborn lamb and pulls out its navel and flies off with all its intestines? Would you be neutral then?'

I was dumb.

'And its t' same wi' t' foxes. They don't just kill for food, they kill for sport. If they get into a henhouse they'll kill thirty or more, bite off their heads and leave them. Just for a game. And they'll take newborn lambs' livers — not eating the whole animal but taking only the delicacy, killing far more than they need.'

'Nearly as bad as people', I said. 'We're not very nice either.'

I was thinking that I'd never heard of foxes using defoliants or napalm, or running concentration camps, or persecuting one another for their beliefs, or even eviscerating and stuffing the animals they had killed, and keeping the corpses about their dens as decoration, nor even keeping boxes of impaled butterflies to give them pleasure, nor building prisons where hens serve life sentences in little boxes wherein they can barely turn round.

' — better dead, from everyone's point of view', the gamekeeper was saying of my crow, not the hens I was thinking about.

'You'll be bringing back capital punishment next', I said.

'I think it should be brought back', he said. 'A murderer knows what he's doing. He knows all about what suffering and misery he's causing.'

'To himself as well, very often; to himself, perhaps, most of all', I thought, but I said — 'That's more than a fox or a carrion crow can know. These creatures are innocently obeying the laws of their own nature.'

'Innocent, are they? A carrion crow will quarter the ground looking for nests. Is it innocent to take the eyes of buried sheep?'

'It is for crows. For them it is not a sheep's eye but a delicious snow-oyster'.

He laughed.

'The crow doesn't give a thought to the sufferings of sheep.'

'But you should — I do — pests must be put down.'

'Aren't we all pests from some creature's point of view? I can't make judgements about who has the right to life.'

'You're being a sentimentalist.'

I hoped not, but he may have been right. My resentment may have indicated that I had been justly hit. But an artist, of any sort, must be neutral; must weigh everything impartially, and live in a condition of acceptance of the shadows: shadows of foxes; shadows of crows gliding over the plover's nest. It is in the shadows that we live. We have our inner shadows too. I know that this attitude inhibits action, and I sometimes feel that instead of all these words, some wordless action is expected of me, but I don't know what it is. So I am helpless — wringing my hands. A sentimentalist.

'You call me sentimentalist. I call you moralist. One cannot take the evil in oneself and project it onto a scapegoat creature — human or otherwise — then hunt it down and kill it, imagining that this cleanses the world.'

This is not what I said, but what I would like to have said. I often find myself running over in my head the conversations I ought to have had, wherein I overstate no cases, make no illogical jumps, and my opponent's arguments are all weak. Both the gamekeeper and I had taken up slightly false positions — he as the Grand Inquisitor, condemning heretic animals, and I as Santa Francesca, championing brother Crow. But Mrs Gamekeeper had arrived, and we were busily papering over the cracks in village relationships with much joking and talk of our various children. There are enough feuds in our village, and only one pub. It is not permissible to quarrel unless one wishes to become a teetotaller.

But as we talked, I was thinking of the crowds of men who assemble for local fox-hunts. They in no way resemble the bowler-hatted horsemen and women of Kent or the West Country; or any other form of Anglo Saxon centaur. They are unspeakable in a different way. They follow the hounds on foot, for this craggy terrain is dangerous for horses, and the hunters aren't usually the sort of people who own horses. They arrive in old Landrovers and battered little vans — they are the hobnailed infantry of hunters, not the cavalry.

Nor do they appear to me much like crusaders against evil. They do not have much idealism shining in their eyes. It is true that, in sheep country, foxes must be controlled, but these hunters are out for sport. They are human foxes and human crows, human hyenas, perhaps, because they laugh much and loudly. Killing is a game.

After the hunt the fox may be hung up by the tail outside the inn, or the gamekeeper's house, to let us all know that the terror of the henhouses is dead; and sometimes there may be a bundle of cubs hung up beside a mangled vixen. Now we can be less careful about fastening the chickens in at night, but there is no less evil in the world.

Sitting Blackbird in a Hawthorn Bush

She neither sings nor displays
but, self absorbed, she will keep
her secret in stillness. Days —
though lengthening — are not long
to her in her watching sleep.
She has withdrawn from time
and hovers above the stream
flowing under the arch of her wing.

A dome of leaves has grown
green over and round the nest
that is the heart of the bush
where the alchemy of her breast
turns past into future thrush.
Within five luminous caves
blind cells of bone align
themselves in appropriate curves
to make next summer's wings.
Tried aerodynamics of time
dictate the form of such things.

Tall grasses rustle up
to meet the trees' low eaves
with walls of buttercup,
cow-parsley, sorrel leaves.
She can almost hear the joints
of extending grass-stems creak
as they rise to attention
for Summer's national anthem
sung, jubilantly, by the lark.

Silent, in mottled shade,
still node in a humming sphere
of bees and insect business
all under a canopy

of music sustained by skylarks,
our bird sits still as a god
who broods in a tree of stars.

The Hawthorn, yesterday,
appeared dusty with blossom,
or else hoar-frosted grey:
the same tree, overnight,
has been visited by white
blizzards of local snow
that, thick as clotted cream,
lie upon her alone.
The tree has snowed from within
not petals, stamens, pistils,
but efflorescent crystals
of hawthorn tree desire.

Still shadow, under opaque
clothing of papery wounds
that bleed aphrodisiac scent,
the sitting bird is immune
to temptation. She's at a work
that resembles prayer; she keeps
the world in repair; she wants
for nothing and does nothing, waits
while cow-parsley erects
its universe of umbels
like model solar systems
whose stalks and spokes are showing.
And Cockbird, on space travels,
skims the galactic meadows
in search of distant heavens.

She draws invisible
mysterious energies
into June's restless landscape
through her obedient eggs.
When metamorphic jellies

have grown wing-buds and legs,
yolk-yellow gapes, and bellies,
hearts, lungs and bruise-blue bulges
that will be eyes; and self-will
enough to crack an eggshell,
they'll peck and push and unpack
themselves into this world.

The hatching of her eggs
divides her happiness
into five separate hungers —
each felt as if her own.
Anxiety begins;
new happiness is work
and active service. Her heart
is scattered until young birds
fare forward autonomously
through the glass wall of Winter
into the mirrored image
of this immortal Summer
where our future is present.

Midsummer Night's Wake

In the Outer Hebrides, even two weeks before midsummer, the sun scarcely dipped under the horizon. It set north-north-west and rose north-north-east. Perhaps for as long as from half past ten until two it was hidden by the curve of the earth, but all night long the sky to the north glowed red and orange as though the Arctic were on fire. Even mid-way between evening and morning it was still fairly light, and after a night of grey dusk full of wakeful birds, the sun used to rouse us in the small hours of the morning. It was not so much a sunrise as a blast-off that we saw as, looked at with only intermittent consciousness, the sun soared into the sky like a rocket, pouring a trail of white fire on the sea.

Because, regrettably, one must sleep, a great deal of best quality morning was wasted. Even here, back in Yorkshire, the day outside the window begins long before I am ready for it, but there has, nevertheless, been a brief but genuine night. On the 21st June the sun set just after nine-thirty, but the night took two hours or more to develop its darkness which, after another hour, began to be diluted by dawn; but we could consider that we had the night back again, and with the night its creatures — bats, moths and hunting owls.

The midsummer night was cold and wild with wind and rain, but midsummer nights since the 21st have been mild and still. It is, I think, this stillness that characterises midsummer. The year has reached the highest point of its parabola, and levels out, preparing for its decline, and as it changes from an upward to a downward progress it must, for a few perfect moments, stand still. Or so it seems.

The trees still have the soft outlines that mean they are yet growing and producing new small leaves, and the fields are soft and rich with standing grass, and, at that point in the dusk when the colours become so intense as to be unidentifiable, like very concentrated dyes, I, quite involuntarily, wait, perfectly still myself, while the wind and the whole world and time itself seem to have stopped, and I become aware of the multitudes of creatures moving in this stillness. The rook community makes one last rowdy parade about the sky then pours, shouting, into its local patch of thicker-woven night — the rookery wood — while, in perfect silence, great white birds are drifting over the hayfield like giant moths. They come quite close and appear, in the dusk, to be headless, like ghosts. Then I see that they are black-headed gulls, gliding to and fro a few feet above the grass, in a kind of ceremony. But this can be no formal dance, birds don't do anything for nothing, even their songs are usually functional announcements of some kind. Then I notice the moths. On invisibly rapid wings, swinging to and fro in a hesitant, zigzagging flight, as though they wish to be taken for white flowers nodding in the wind (but there is no wind), they travel on their momentous journeys out of and over the grass, and back into the grass again, if they are lucky. For the drifting gulls are hunting the moths and catching them on the wing, like swallows or swifts.

I remember that some years ago my children had two pet white ducks, and these used to run to and fro on their rubbery orange feet, jumping into the air after the moths. They found it well worthwhile to stay up late to perform this evening ballet, which looked very funny from a distance. And our cat, too, has been known to perform like Nijinsky, jumping for moths.

As dark as the moths and gulls are pale, a bat flitters rapidly overhead. Between the larches in the plantation up the lane, the numerous population of bats makes its swift, criss-crossing, apparently panic-stricken dashes across patches of lighter sky between darkness and darkness. I can see but not hear them, although my young son assures me that they squeak, and I can hear but not see a distant owl. But night by no means belongs to the officially nocturnal. The rooks seem to be having a party in their wood. Every now and then it reaches a quarrelsome climax. A curlew's alarm call pierces the night. Lapwings are still up, and vocal, somewhere along a ridge of the hills where pale, newly-shorn sheep are bleating. A mile away across the dale behind me is the limeworks, rumbling, rattling and shaking down its clinker all night. Men are not really nocturnal either, but our adaptability is one of the secrets of our success, as it is of the success of gulls living inland. And we outdo the gulls, as we adapt our environment as well as ourselves. The quarry nibbles the moor away. But I myself am not quite adaptable enough to stay awake any longer.

The Martin's Nest

I can still remember quite clearly the first book I ever read. It was about a stone-age child (with whom it was very easy to identify, as all children are primitive beings), who made adventurous forays from the parental tree-house and discovered various things. He discovered fire when a tree was struck by lightning, and one of its uses when he saw that wild animals were afraid of it. This made cave-dwelling possible. Then he found that meat tasted better when slightly burnt. He discovered clay in the river-bank, and how plastic and obedient it was. He played with it and rolled it into snakes between the palms of his hands. He wound the snakes into snails, saucers, basins and pots. Then, using these vessels for trying to keep his bits of meat clean while cooking them in the fire, he discovered that these objects were made permanent if they fell into the fire and became red hot. So he invented rudimentary pottery.

But now, I have decided that my first book was mistaken. This stone-age boy, whose name may have been Ug, did not stumble, almost by accident, upon the art of pottery. He had teachers. The birds were on earth before mankind, and the martins — which, at that time must have been called cave martins, not house martins — were already making pots. Ug simply observed them building their nests under the overhanging ledges of the family grotto, and then imitated them. I came to this conclusion in mid-May of this year, when the martins arrived and started building just outside our new window. The first prospectors noticed a very slight ridge in the stonework, high up, about ten inches below the lintel, and from this slight encouragement, they built. There were more than two of them shuttling to and fro. Perhaps the cock bird had two wives, or perhaps it was a small commune. Certainly there were always crowds of martins by the muddy puddles at the bottom of the lane, scooping up beak-fulls of mud and marking the soft ground with beaks and delicate feet, though in constant danger from a tigerish ginger cat that lurked in the budding hedgerow, and whose bird-watching was far from disinterested.

Up at our end of the shuttle service, the birds made first a bracket, then a half-saucer, then a balcony. When they built up one side of the balcony higher than the other, it looked as though they were making mistakes, but they all knew exactly what they were doing. Somewhere inside each bird's skull a well-worked-out blueprint was folded. The higher side of the nest curved regularly up and over to meet the underside of the lintel, and then the large opening close to the window was filled, until there was only enough room for one martin to slip in or out at a time. This martin-pot had been built from the inside, so that, once its sides began to grow, only the head of the crafts-bird could be seen at work, raising the walls of this neat hanging oven for the cooking up of eggs into little martins.

'They'll make a dreadful mess on your window; knock it down', said almost everyone, but we didn't mind. The martins were a symbol of summer, and it was worth a little mess to have them so close. Although, having become martin-conscious, when I noticed barns with whole rows of martins' nests under their eaves, it did appear to be like an infestation, or a house with cysts.

There was a fairly quiet period when the egg-laying and the incubation must have taken place, until one morning we found the fragile halves of four or five small white eggs on the sill below the nest. Then the to-ing and fro-ing began again, but this time the arrival of a parent bird with a beakful was greeted by a chorus of appreciative shrilling. The young birds began to appear at the entrance hole, and when they had been fed they would turn around and spatter our window with the droppings that everyone had warned us about. We began to wonder when this ordeal was going to end. The rearing of young martins seemed to be an interminable task. They already looked perfectly airworthy as they peered out at the world, wearing full evening dress for life's party, but with their white shirt-tails hanging out.

At last, on the 20th July, the nest had become very quiet, and a blizzard of birds whirled about over our croft. They had just discovered that they had a genius for flight. Effortlessly as self-propelled kites they circled, undulating as though they rode on an invisible big dipper of the air, round and round, very fast, with intermittent flapping of the wings. They were very beautiful, very joyous: it must have been a great relief to be out of the now very tight-fitting earth womb, although they still re-entered the old slum occasionally, and possibly roosted there. But we decided not to let them get going on a second brood, and a few days after the family was fledged we fixed up a ladder and knocked the nest down.

I had expected to be able to pick up a few pieces, like potsherds. I had hoped to take a close look at the technique of these no-handed potters. But, once dislodged, the nest that had appeared to be so substantial simply crumbled to powder. There was a little dry moss and a few chicken feathers by way of a mattress, but of the martins' home, now that it had fulfilled its function, there was nothing left but a handful of dust, as though it was only the necessity for its existence that kept it together.

Tewitts

In spring and early summer there have always been plenty of green plovers about, but we have never had them nesting just over the wall from our kitchen-garden before. This year, during April, we heard their cries about our hilltop far into the evenings and well after dark, and could watch them seeing rooks and other crows off the premises of their territorial air-space from our bedroom window in the mornings.

We had a grandstand view of their stunt flying in crazy courtship display, which seems to confirm the Ancient Greek unnatural history of the origin of plovers, which, like so many classical explanations of 'the mystery of mysteries', follow an anti-evolutionary pattern, so that a human being becomes a bird, a tree, a bat, or, perhaps, some famous man-shaped stone.

The lapwing story concerns Daedalus, the father of Icarus, the boy for whom he made wings which fell to bits in mid-air, so he dropped into the sea and was drowned. This early scientist has something a little sinister about him, for he also had a nephew who worked with him as an inventor's apprentice. The nephew roused his uncle's jealousy by out-inventing him, so that Daedalus could stand it no longer and flung the lad to his death from a high tower. This may, of course, have been another experiment in flight, but, in any case, Pallas Athene, patron goddess of clever men, took pity on the gifted boy and, just before he hit the ground, unfolded for him a great spread of wings and turned him into the first plover, or 'tewitt' as they are called locally; so plovers, or tewitts, or peewits, or lapwings, have been reliving this traumatic experience ever since.

But the apparently uncontrolled fall out of the sky is not the only performance our plovers have repeated this year. The lateness of haytime, because of the rain, has allowed them to rear a second brood of young.

A fortnight ago, in late June, they were fussing about over the field next door, and behaving in that shrill plover-like manner which only attracts attention to that from which they are trying to distract us, so that we waded a little way into the grass — which still upholsters the fields and the roadsides — and found two innocently bleeping chicks within a few yards of each other, tunnelling about through the grass forest. They were mottled and marbled with brown, grey-black, khaki and whitish fluff, and as well camouflaged as the eggs from which they had recently emerged. They had a ring of white round their necks, intelligently shining dark eyes, and a wader's long legs folded under them. They were already well able to travel through the meadow and moorland grass. Their parents, and an older brother or sister in brownish juvenile plumage, shrieked overhead, and their disturbance disturbed us, so we left the chicks to the business of growing up, and hope that they succeed in becoming strong on the wing before our neighbours 'drop the meadows'. The bruise-dark rain clouds still sweeping in over Ingleborough are on their side, but mortality must be considerable. Apart from the hazards of nature, there is, these days, the possibility of death on the road.

Several times in the last few weeks I have seen, from the car, long-legged plover chicks walking in the gutter, and two or three days ago — out walking — we picked up a juvenile bird, still warm, that must have been smacked by a passing car at the very outset of its flying career. Having made, owing to youthful inexperience, a fatal miscalculation, all its subtle camouflage, all the trouble it had taken to become this intricate, highly evolved flying machine, and all its parents' many weeks of anxious care, were suddenly rendered useless. But its deadness gave us a chance to take a close look at it.

The feathers of its mud-brown mantle were fringed with gold, the colour of bleached sedges, and its lesser and median wing-coverts were tiled with tiny iridescent green feathers, smooth as silk. It wore viridian and spinach greens, and the green of moorland rivers reflecting trees. Its head was still mottled like its eye-deceiving egg, and there were touches of earthy red and areas of cloud-white. Its colours were those of our landscape, as though, in it, Ribblesdale had concentrated and painted itself with its own blood, to fly out of itself and become aware of itself and thus, alas, to suffer — for the parent birds were crying overhead.

But a flock of more than twenty tewitts flew up from a field by the road as we walked on, for the lapwings have done well this year, and are entering the time when they cut their losses and flock together into the August silence.

Weeds

Alone (with the children) for a few weeks, I discover that the freedom of solitude is an illusion. There may be a little less to do, but there are fifty per cent less people doing it. Individual cells are an uneconomical social unit as, in them, one person has to do twice as many chores for half as many people. In spite of stresses and tensions, the larger unit gives a good deal more freedom, and also provokes more action. We strike various sparks off one another.

Yet solitude, also, tends to provoke action, as one may feel compelled to justify one's existence creatively. I do not find it possible to be satisfied by a scheme of things in which one eats and sleeps in order to eat and sleep, but it is possible to sit back and feel that life is raised above the existence level by the work of a husband, or even by the work of children; but alone, with children at school all day, I must do it myself. So I sit down and write poetry, and I read, and I write more, and I become lost in the world of the imagination. Then I look up.

Larks are singing midsummer outside, but inside is sunk in green subaqueous gloom. The reason for this is that while deep in thought, or writing, or else scurrying round tidying up after myself (and children), the garden has been knitting itself up into a green summer garment for the house. It has risen outside the windows as though we are sinking in a vegetable sea. Ferns lean their curved, tapering ladders against the window, and red-veined rose leaves press against the glass. Honeysuckle scrambles about, looking for support, forsythia branches droop before the window: the whole garden appears to be about to come in.

I grope my way out, through ivy, and once outside I see that the lawn has sprung up like one of those mythical armies that grow after the planting of dragon's teeth, or stones, in ancient Greek stories. 'I must do battle', I mutter, thinking 'so this is what they mean by a "grass widow"', and 'reverence for life can go too far', and fetch the infernal machine which is supposed to be an improvement on a mower, I pour in petrol and I pull the string. The machine sulks; but at this point the children come home from school, and they take over. They are modern, technological children; they like machines and understand their psychology. They can coax them to respond to starting mechanisms, and they can even get them to stop, once started. So they do the lawn, and I bend to the weeding.

'These must be what they mean by "widow's weeds"', I think, looking at the chandeliers of golden flowers that hang upwards out of the earth in response to the gravitational pull of the sun. I look at the rosettes of serrated leaves, and I look at the grass plumes spiking up through Siberian chickweed, tiny wild geraniums, buttercups, plantains, dandelions and daisies. The vegetable garden is like a hayfield. The usual groundsel is crowded out by more ambitious plants. Fireweed is setting up its towers, and the bindweed is attacking them. So I attack the bindweed, the fireweed, the grass, dandelions, buttercups, and countless coarse and anonymous lower orders of weeds. With both hands I grasp the tough and sappy stalks, I wrench up roots, and, in the name of order, I lay waste. I dig and grub and chop and hoe until I am tired, and then the doubt that has been growing like a weed in my mind voices itself.

'By what right do you destroy these lives?' I ask myself. 'You, who couldn't create one miserable groundsel flower, are destroying all these beautiful beings. What right have you to decide that this row of puny carrots shall live and these splendid thistles shall die? Why should these neglected, greenfly-laden roses be allowed to live while these vigorous and healthy buttercups are condemned? Is this not to play God? And how do you know, in any case, that these plants do not suffer?' I consider the evidence that they do: their thorns and stings for self-protection; their ability to die of shock. I think of the earth-healing power of weeds — that they grow over quarries, disused kilns, ruined buildings and derelict machines, and bind them to the earth again. I think of the old quarry at Stainforth: how its ledges are colonised by hawthorns and mountain ashes, and its slag-heaps clothed with wild flowers. In the cracks of the brickwork of the old kiln grow grass, campions, thistles, marguerites, escaped garden flowers (various), and wild strawberries. These last send out reconnaissant runners like tacking stitches from crevice to crevice, and insert new plants. The slanting walls of crumbling brickwork suit them well. Very recently the quarry has been used by the council as an answer to the rubbish tipping problem. Dustcarts are laying down the plastic levels for future geologists to uncover and puzzle over; but having seen the quarry begin to heal I know it can do so again. The wilderness returns and hides our squalor. It can even beat concrete, in time.

But gardening is not squalid. Gardening is human order in the anarchic wilderness. It is an invited party of plants, and, in order that it can be enjoyed, gatecrashers must be excluded by weeding. 'Besides, nothing is really destroyed', I think, bending my back to ruthless hoeing once again. Even though we may succeed in eradicating the bindweed, a little weeding does not 'crack nature's moulds', or spill all germens at once. Weeding is not genocide, unless carried to extreme excess. These vigorous and cheerful weeds are like a Chinese festival of traditional paper kites, masks, beasts, dragons and flowers; immortal art in a temporary material. They are all destructible, but also eternal, for the ancient designs will be used again to make these flimsy forms for next year's festival. It doesn't matter that they are all burned when the festival is over: their patterns exist.

I thank heaven for this earthly immortality, for I love weeds. I remember a wood full of red campions, white stitchwort and bluebells on a coronation day, when I was a child. 'How patriotic of them', I thought then; and weeds are patriotic. They do a good deal for the country. The wilderness is as necessary to us as is order. It is the gold-reserve of the earth's vitality; but it, too, needs us, for 'without man, nature is barren', as Blake said, because it has no awareness of itself. Through us nature looks at herself and sees that she is beautiful; and she is made more beautiful by the bright geometry of cultivation.

Butterfly Worksong

To be a butterfly is no light matter;

with glittering rapidity we flutter
huge sails like airborne windmills, stop the motor

and drill for nectar wells, then, like blown litter,
we putter off again. We are the porters

in wild art galleries, and shift exhibits
from dandelions, or thistle-topmost summits,

to gardens in the humans' walled-in quarters.
Each diptych lifts its labouring transporter

which, inadvertently, in course of duty,
must pollinate the flowers where, blind to beauty,

we top up fuel tanks of honey-water.
Much put-upon, we batter wings to tatters,

and if we take time off to understand
our purposes, the shadow of a hand

destroys our quivering rest. Don't think us flighty;
we dance like sparks to rearrange the weighty

midsummer exhibition: bear the garden
on shoulders bowed beneath their gaudy burden

of abstract canvases by the Almighty.

Curlew in July

She walks the wall on bamboo bones
and stands on sentry-duty, and she warns
her children of the holocaust machines.

Once in the days of scythe and rake,
these meadows were the Kingdom of the Crake.

Now tractors rage all round the field
and mower-blades bite stems, and swathes are felled
to sigh to earth while crouching birds are killed.

The Curlew circles, shrieking panic Morse,
returning later to assess her loss.

She voices her shrill queries from the wall,
and shriller pipes respond. Perhaps not all
her chicks, but one plus one, alive and well,

extend their necks to peer above the stubble
like periscopes, but aren't yet out of trouble.

They must survive the siderake, and outlast
the deadcart silage box till it's gone past,
but there are patches where the Corncrake's ghost

still haunts: beside a barn, a knoll too steep
for tractors, and a smear where mud's too deep,

so there Grass Forest stands, and one plus one
may hide while Jackdaws forage on the crown
of Curlew Hill as this day's sun goes down.

If they avoided Undertaker Crow,
at dawn, on fragile legs, the fledgelings go

uphill to pastureland. On wall-top stones
the mother stalks along on bamboo bones
and splits her beak to utter warning tones

and lullabies and food-calls, and express
anxiety; her love is half distress
and latent sorrow; such is happiness.

Haytime

The grass stood tall and still in the fields. Each little hill had a soft outline as though clothed in a rich fur coat that, instead of moulting, grew thicker every day as the grasses reached sunward, and the sorrel flowers pushed up through buttercups and marguerites to give the fields a toasted look. So it was not a green fur coat but a gold and russet coloured one that, though full of moths, mice, voles, leverets, skylarks, meadow-pipits and yellow wagtails grew continually more and more beautiful and valuable.

When the breeze stirred it, it seemed alive, as, of course, it was; and when it stood still it seemed to be full of a most exemplary serenity, although awaiting execution, for it was ripe for mowing. In a barn nearby, our neighbour sharpened the triangular teeth of the mower blades, and tractors and balers were fettled up. Then there was only the weather to wait for.

One exceptionally still dusk, while the hills wrapped themselves in mist, I was watching the moth-hunting gulls dipping into the sea of grass, reminding me of terns diving. I could hear the dry splash of wings floundering in grass, and I could hear very little else, when from a hillside half a mile away grew the drone of a tractor. Headlamps glared round the hillside, dazzling, and the tractor descended the field to disappear behind the hedge of trees. The lights flashed out intermittently from between the trees, then they and the tractor climbed up the third side of the meadow, to hide behind the drumlin hill. 'They must be feeling very sure of the weather', I thought, and they were, and they were right, for since then everyone, on every flawless day, has been making hay.

The tractors hum like bees in Ribblesdale. I wake to their sound, and the shrill ringing of mowing machines, and get up to the smell of mown grass. I am also wakened, equally early, by a thrush who sits on a nest in the clematis beside my window. When I first spotted this bird, I was not perfectly certain whether she had built a nest or a hide for observing mad humans, for the bird sat all day up there in her bower, and, every time I looked up at her, I caught her astonished eye, looking at me. Just about the time when the mowing began, the eggs must have hatched out, for now there is much to-ing and fro-ing of parent birds with beaks full of grubs, slugs, moths and other delicacies from the grass. One or other of the birds still sits on the nest from time to time, to warm and protect the young, and, as they grow and sprout feathers, a regally maternal thrush rises up on a fidgeting tide of scraggy necks, gaping beaks, fluttering wings and still naked rumps. As the nestlings gain in size and physical competence, they put in quite a lot of time preening and scratching. Nest life must be pretty itchy, as well as crowded. After a fortnight, the young birds, able to stand it no longer, clamber to the edge of the nest to digest some of the countless courses of their continuous meals, to exercise their wings, and to look sleepily out on the great world where mad ladies talk to birds and, in the middle distance, tractors continually spiral round fields.

Thus they have a grandstand view of this beautiful heatwave haytime, and could see, had they not dozed off, the restless grass suddenly stilled and laid out in rows. Gulls and rooks walk about the fields eating the now accessible denizens of the grass forest, and mercifully polishing off any voles, chicks, and other small creatures that may have been cut by the mower. The orderly rows of the felled grass are tossed about, sun-dried, and raked into rows again to be baled into blocks by the grunting baler, its tireless elbow packing tight the summer for winter use. Field after field is mown, dried, baled and carted home to the barns, from dawn until well after dark, when the moon rises huge and pinkish-gold to stare on the great loads, nine bales high, that sway slowly down the lane like hairy double-decker buses.

Now it is all but done. The hay is in, and none of it has been spoiled. Nor has work been wasted. But not only is next winter's hay secure, but also, where a few weeks ago there were only two thrushes, there are now six, and this was probably due to a second brood. So next year's thrush supply has also been laid in.

Hedge

In austere drystone-wall country I sometimes find myself pining for the hedges of my childhood which, as I peer backwards at them through the rose-tinted magnifying glass of memory, were pillared with great oaks or elms, pilastered with foxgloves, wallpapered with wild roses, honeysuckles and hawthorn. Then, later in the year, the hedges became bursting larders of blackberries, hips, haws and wild apples, as well as those beautiful and extra glossy bryonys we were well warned not to taste.

Walking between white roadside walls through the high bleakness of Upper Ribblesdale, and thinking of those hedges, it appeared to me that the fields above the road had been building walls of their own, one beyond another; for the hillside ascended like stairs, and broken-off bedding planes of limestone lifted the turf at every riser. On the highest of these natural walls occasional rowans, sloes, hawthorns and ashes were growing, rooted in rock and out of reach of sheep, but they did not amount to a hedge. Hedges must be exuberant with excess, ungroomed and tending to wilderness, not clinging for dear life to unfriendly crags. Then, in the far distance, past the tarn and over the undulations of drumlins, I see a dark fuzz by the road. Unkempt and spreading over roadside verges, invading fields, is a few hundred yards of real hedge.

On reaching it I find it full of sloe bushes, two ancient crab apple trees, some great ashes and convoluted hawthorns. Thickets of rosehips are reddening, and haws are ripening brownishly. Amid the dishevelled scruffiness of late summer knapweed and yarrow, long grasses, ragwort and a few blue scraps of harebell all succeed in looking as though they have been trampled by a great cow. There is too much wealth here: plant overlaid on plant. Goosegrass scrambles up twigs and brambles lean on tree-roots which grip the ruins of an overthrown wall.

Some thistledowns drift past on a light wind. They may anchor and add to next year's confusion, but do not seem ready to settle yet. I catch one and try to look at it, but each time I open my fingers it escapes. Recapturing it I do manage to hold it long enough to see that every silken filament of this spherical flying-machine is divided and divided to an almost invisible fineness. The radiating hairs are hairy, in fact, and, catching the wind, the thistledown darts off again. Now, hovering up and down in a similar way, a tortoiseshell butterfly drifts from amongst the exhausted ranks of nettles that grow in the ditch and defend the apple tree. It settles on a roadside stone and spreads its wings out flat to catch the sun, as though it fed on light. At a shadow's touch it flutters away, but settles on a wall and once again spreads out its coloured cloak. You may look at it as closely as you like so long as your shadow doesn't fall on it. Look at its fluorescent orange, like a roadman's jacket; at its symmetry, its ragged edge, its alert antennae, the hairiness of its body spreading out over the roots of its wings; look at its borders of misty-blue spots, of a colour exactly complementary to the butterfly's prevailing tawniness. It is a masterpiece of design that is made of nettles, for its larvae feed on these: it is perfection from the weediest of coarse and ragged weeds.

Surprises

I remember being told by a teacher, long ago, that 'intelligent people are never surprised', and if she meant that it is simple-minded to be surprised by the terrible things people can do to one another, she may have been right, for one doesn't need to be alive and awake for very long to observe what sort of thing mankind is liable to get up to. But if one takes too dim a view of humanity one may be surprised by goodness, and this is foolish also.

I myself am often surprised, but principally by the behaviour of vegetables, and I enjoy my folly. It is the meek strength of plants that astonishes me, as does the ingenuity of many in finding a root-hold in this crowded world. I have seen sycamore seedlings growing on the tops of walls and in the forks of other trees, and doormats of dandelions on the steps of empty cottages that are gift-wrapped up in knots of honeysuckle string. I am surprised by the sleeping beauty, rosebay willowherb, that can lie buried under cities for a hundred years, and at the persistence of weeds in the face of weeding, their refusal to despair, and their repeated attempts to forgive concrete, tarmac and paving-stones.

I am not only surprised by the weeds in our garden, I am also surprised by the legitimate plants. We have an amazing cherry tree which is a memento of a distant summer day when the children were tiny and we sat outside eating cherries and flinging the stones about. 'We'll have a cherry tree there', we said, tossing a pip; and there it is now, twelve years later, twice as tall as we are.

Gardening tends to surprise because it is a game one plays with time as a playfellow, and time has a way of hiding things and then bringing them to light again later, just when he pleases. Besides, when I plant things I am rather like a dog burying bones, and forget what I have put where.

We had forgotten that the children planted a marrow before we went away on holiday. After our return we were all lost in astonishment at the marrow-jungle proliferating all over the garden. It sends out long branches to overrun the strawberries and to snake about between the surprising football-sized cabbages that were supposed to be brussel sprouts. It curls and tangles its green bedspring tendrils, it spreads enormous ragged leaves, it opens gaping yellow craters into which bees bravely descend. And, surprise of surprises, it is actually producing marrows. Not only are these marrows huge, they daily, even hourly, grow huger. And they look so professional. They are not at all the sort of blighted product I expect from our garden.

I have also been surprised, lately, by a briar rose. At first I thought it must have been brought by a bird, but then I remembered planting a rose-bush of some cabbagey cultivated kind. I ought to have known, but I didn't, that roses revert to briar unless all growth from below the graft is removed. It wasn't removed, it flourished, and I thought that my rose did well, but the golden cabbage lost heart and vanished. Hence the pale wild rose that bloomed so well in July, and hence the scarlet hips that gleam in the garden now. It may not have been brought by a bird, but its very large and brilliant berries certainly bring the birds to the bush. Amid much rustling and shaking of leaves, a brown-speckled juvenile blackbird is busy jerking the berries from the boughs. Having succeeded in picking a berry, the bird sits on the fence-post with a gleaming ruby carbuncle in its bill, then suddenly swallows it whole. Even the bird seems a little surprised, but returns for more, so it doesn't die of indigestion, which is also surprising.

Even the banal fact that like breeds like surprises me; that every rosehip contains numerous seeds, each containing the knowledge of how to be a briar rose bush, makes me dumb with astonishment. Each individual pip knows how to make root and shoot, how to spin petal and leaf, how to pack both petals and leaves in buds, and how to open those buds in response to the sun. If one rosehip were to be saved intact from a worldwide holocaust, the whole world would, before long, be a briar thicket (provided that there were also some bees, and perhaps a bird or two).

This invisible knowledge packed into berries, pods and nuts is what amazes me most. In every dustgrain of seed, in every shrunken and trepanned head of the poppy, in every snowflake of the rosebay storm, in every pellet shot from broom-pods in the sun, is packed the incommunicable secret of how to be itself.

Bat Poem

Bat poems should be written black on black
then black on evening light
when torn triangular wing-writing makes
cursive, quickflickering remarks
along the edge of night.

Ninety per cent unseen, mysterious,
they should be a continuous-
ly vanishing surprise,
from pockets of invisibility
materialise
showing anarchic unpredictability
of line-length, disappearing as we stare
into the oval window of the moon,
into thin air.

Illogical, tangential,
they should make sudden dashes after moth
or beetle thoughts
while trawling dusk for truth
or gnats
or both.

They may appear to magnify
moths' orange underwings,
craneflies,
deep ashtree sighs,
distorting fair proportion between things,
for Flittermouse and Noctule's fingerbones
are longer than their thighs.

Bat poems should be silent,
listening,
their gargoyle faces funnelling
the echoes of their own

stuttering decibels
home to the signal drums of Pipistrelles.

For they perceive by hearing
dancing swarms,
cockchafers, humans loitering alone,
tree-shadows by the lane;
their soundless sound must conjure solid forms
clear on mind's radar screen.

Anarchists

The armies of grass stand in the fields, buttercup-brass helmeted and foxtail plumed, armed with green-blade bayonets and seeds for bullets, and supported by underground movements of roots, awaiting zero-hour. When it strikes, the mowers cut down these unresisting armies that cannot run, lacy camp-following flowers and all, leaving swathes of dead on the stubble to desiccate in the sun. Instead of stretcher-parties to seek among the bodies for any left living, the tedders come and toss the grass about to make sure that it all dies, so that no spark of life can smoulder in the midst of the stacked hay. Then the side-rakes swish the dry grass into military rows, and the dead-carts come and bear it away to the barns. From early to late, men are in the fields, making hay while the sun shines, and often when it doesn't, snatching their harvest from the uncertain season.

The grass offers no gesture of resistance to the devouring machines of its death, nor to the unsentimental farmer who whistles as the summer collapses in the field. It lies down and dies in the prime of its beauty, but though this army of summer is slain, nothing is dead, but all will be here again next year — all the immortal green multitude and the hosts of gold buttercups and rusty sorrel flowers, the lacy cow-parsley and meadowsweet.

The winter kills it and it is greener than ever in spring; the cattle devour it, and it flourishes on their dung; men plough it up, but it creeps back undefeated; men build on it and it grows over their buildings; we mow it and entomb it, but the grass still inherits the earth. It is an invincible non-resisting army, and it reminds me of that other army which has, so far, never been beaten: the anarchist army of women.

It is armed with prams for tanks, playpens for palisades, breadknives for bayonets, and brooms and buckets and mops and brushes for general terror, and it goes into battle with a baby under one arm and a bundle of nappies under the other, with batteries of blandishments, arsenals of energy and reinforcements of self discipline. Its tactics are gentleness and its headquarters are love. It is clad in the colourful non-uniform of individuality, decorated by coquetry, and in it every private is a major general.

The work of every other army — even the most efficient desolation-making machines — is patiently undone in twenty years by the anarchist army of women, with ovaries full of ammunition and strings of white bunting hung out over back-yards in token of every minor victory.

'Life is indestructible', sings the new spring grass, and the napkins on the line, and the newborn babies wailing.

But now the enemy armies, rallied by our urge to death, have found a new weapon — genetic damage by radiation — which carries the battle within the very gates of the anarchist citadel. They have found out how to poison the source of life, and to make caricatures of the victories of women. So now it remains to be seen whether this unorganised rabble of a chattering army of life can still triumph over the well-disciplined cohorts of scientifically organised death. If not, the green armies of meek grass may march, invading our cities and setting their flags on our battlements, in token of the victory of the unintelligent and inhuman.

Following Summer

When haytime is over the summer seems to be over, too. Certainly its climax is past, for the grass will never be so tall again, nor will it have that air of urgent growth about it. Yet the elder trees were still smothered with fragrant, cream-coloured lace, and the meadowsweet was blooming in the lane when term ended and we decamped to follow summer northward.

It is a fallacy to think that one can follow the summer south, for in southern Europe the best of the season is over in May, and what tourists find in August is a tyrannical sun's scorched earth policy. Even river-beds are dried up, and water rises mainly in disguise — as melons, pumpkins or grapes — and shade shrinks and hides indoors or under vines. This is not summer, but the reign of terror of an over-powerful sun. Summer lies to the North where the long days are.

In the Hebrides in late July we found ourselves back in June, partly because the sheep go up the hills very late, and any flowers to show their faces in May are promptly nibbled off. So May, June and July break out together in a summer with a difference. For orchids, primroses, kingcups, buttercups, campions and seapinks all nod together on the machair, their colours dimmed by the viridian and ultramarine of the neighbouring sea.

I suppose it would be possible, these days, to follow summer all the year round, even to the antipodes, which would be like spending one's life in a perpetual adolescence, or courtship, or honeymoon, which may seem desirable but isn't, because a stuck gramophone needle is a stuck gramophone needle, and reiteration of the same phrase, however sweet, spoils the music and stops the dance. Life is change. Things move on. A dance cannot stand still. There is a time to sow and a time to reap, a time to be born and a time to die, and so on; as we all know. There is a time for spring and a time for t' back-end, and that is now. We grow tired of summer, even as the summer grows tired of itself.

So, returning to Horton-in-Ribblesdale, we exchange a stony landscape wearing vivid scarves of sea for this valley that wears an intense green velvet lining of after-grass.

The meadowsweet has transformed itself into spiralling green seeds, and the elderflowers have become hard green berries on red stems. The last of the rosebay willowherb blossoms cling to the tops of their tall fire escapes, all but superseded by the tawdry gold of ragwort encampments, but the dominant colour about us is still this unbelievable green. We pay the price for so much greenness by enduring days and nights of lashing rain that bring the becks out into beer-brown and frothy flood. The steps of rock at Douk Ghyll cave are altogether hidden by the thundering smother of waterfalls, and the racing water undulates over covered boulders and trims the underside of the huge and ancient horse-chestnut near the school. This is, as usual, the first tree to be tinged by autumn.

The Paper City

At about midsummer I noticed what I at first thought was a swallows' nest clinging to the underside of our high studio-door lintel. A second look told me that the cement-coloured protuberance was a wasps' nest, but this was more or less a guess, as I had never seen one before. I remembered having seen a queen wasp, in April, going snipper-snapper among last year's raspberry canes. She had sounded like a certain much-advertised breakfast cereal, or the kindling of a twig fire. I soon traced the sound to the large wasp which, in the very breakfast-time of the year, was gathering wood fibre for her paper-making operation. She was about to lay the foundations of her summer palace. Later, the first-born workers would continue the building to house her thousand children.

As June turned into July, and July to August, the neat whorl of the nest became a greyish inverted turban, a bandaged head, a very dead cabbage, a tumour on the beam. Visitors cried out with horror at it and said we would be stung to death, but we lived in perfect peace with our lodgers who went about their daily business outside while we went about ours within. Wasps are not like houseflies; they take little interest in humanity unless we are making jam, and they are clean and wholesome in their habits. They are not gratuitously aggressive towards people, and sting us only in self-defence.

Humans who flap newspapers at wasps, or go berserk with fly-sprays all over the picnic food, are much more of a menace than this urbane and elegant insect, with its glittering wings, scissoring mandibles, armoured thorax, and middle waisted away to a mere isthmus between jacket and tiger-striped bustle. Wasps are less destructive of human substance than cabbage-white butterflies, rabbits, or plagues of pigeons encouraged by old ladies in towns. Live and let live, said I in this case.

In early September, after several wet weeks and one or two slight frosts, all activity in the cement-grey excrescence seemed to have ceased. No more dead wasps were to be found on the doorstep, there were no more comings and goings at the round hole that pierced the multiple paper walls, and it was some time since any wasps had been at work along the edges of the paper cabbage's outside leaves, adding their fee for life to the wrappings of the mysterious gift within. So I thought it was high time to harvest this summer's growth. I fetched a ladder and a paint-scraper and, supporting the soft and flimsy udder with my left hand, I scraped at its attachment to the underside of the stone lintel with my right. Soon the whole bundle was detached, without being too much dented, and I climbed down the ladder with it.

Looked at closely, the stone-grey paper was a lovely composite of grey, silver and greenish stripes, each one being made of different sorts of wood, some of it mossy, so each wasp's contribution had dried out a different colour. The paper had a faint silkiness, but it was very absorbent, like the softest of soft toilet-rolls, of almost the goose-neck texture that Rabelais extolled.

I bore away this floppy parcel, reflecting that I held a defunct civilisation in my hands. I intended to dissect it, for I had to know what it contained, though I suppose I might have lit the fire with it. I imagined a mass of papery leaves right through to its papery heart, and expected to find that the dead wasps and grubs had lived between its layers. So I scissored carefully into it, as though cutting a quarter out of a cabbage, and I anticipated the discovery of corpses at every snip. But, having gone through about twelve layers of paper, I discovered that the inverted dome was hollow, and I was in the heart of the wasps' collective womb.

Within its shadowy cave was a tree-like structure in four hexagonal layers, rather like a simplified cedar, but this tree would have grown downwards from its root. The suspended storeys were linked by a trunk of papier mâché, and were composed of empty hexagonal cells where infant wasps had matured. Crouched at the edge of the latest and smallest floor, still brooding over her countless cradles, and still poised to lay yet another egg, was the venerable queen. She had died on the job. Round the rim of this newest area, many of the close-packed egg-boxes were still sealed with paper blisters covering the unhatched dead. They had set out too late to catch the summer and had missed the bus of life forever. So cradles became coffins.

The whole tableau made me feel that I and my scissors had intruded upon a holy mystery wherein the gods were still at their work of creating the everlasting future: yet it was also a necropolis. Summer's city had met disaster: the neutron bomb of frost.

The Sunflowers

With laiking southerners' extravagance
I sowed this northern hill with sunflowerseed,
though sighing ash and thorn might scorn the dance
of heliotropic-tilting leaf and head.

I shivered in my exile, (Spring delayed),
and longed to grow tall vegetable suns,
an infant god's flame bonnet, self-portrayed:
a troupe of haloed clowns.

Devotedly I watered, through May's drought,
twin cotyledons, cunningly tugged out
of splitting husks, to balance on one foot
and juggle with the light.

They drank, through June, the grey incessant rain
and fed their cordate rags on cold and wet;
by twos and threes, leaves clambered toward noon
long after noon, and no bloom budded yet.

None flowered when September gales laid waste;
reclined, oblique, my solar totems lay:
but each raised a defiant, green-clawed fist,
and each fist held an eye.

These spiky hands were heads, and all their minds
were compound lenses, wrapped in eyelash fringe,
till straight through Winter's ruined borderlands
a south wind breathed on each stiff petal-hinge.

Slowly they splash the dusk with wheels of flame
to bear me through the dark; grave offerings:
coronas of eclipse, at curfew time:
the tattered paper crowns of beggar kings.

Clouds & Hills (1961)

Where Has the Summer Gone?

The trees are tired of their burden of leaves. All their greens have darkened and turned brownish. The sycamore's flapping sails, manufactured from sunlight all summer long, are heavy and leathery; the beech leaves have lost their suppleness and become set in their ways; the ashes, laden with bunches of yellowing keys, are tinged with copper. Not yet brilliant with autumn, the landscape is tarnished, and melancholy with fatigue. Summer cannot hold on any longer.

Above rain-sodden fields the sky is grey with more rain to come, and heavy tears drip from twigs, leaf-tips, blown roses, ripening fruit. The martins that, a few days ago, waited for their southbound trains along the station platforms of the telegraph wires, have now departed. Their train is always on time, for it is time itself that carries them away. They do not have to feel the unkind hinting of frost before they go. The days can be mild and invite them to stay; the air can be hazy with insects: but as soon as the days begin to be short the martins must go. The great train of time brings the equinox and sweeps them from their airy stations.

So we are left to mourn in this sad landscape, knowing that summer is really dead, although the comfrey plant in the garden has produced a second crop of leaning leafy towers, unfolding 'more and yet more later flowers for bees', just as though it weren't. Yet warm days cease, for on one or two evenings last week the bees were caught out by a sharp drop in temperature near sundown, so that they fell asleep still clinging to the dropping teats of the flowers, like infants falling asleep at the breast. And in the morning they were still there — black clusters of comatose bees hanging under the comfrey flowers. If one breathed gently on them they would stir, drowsily; and the sun restored them to life. But a night frost would have killed them where they slept, and an overcast morning would have failed to rouse them. So they would have been as finished as summer itself.

To shake off this autumnal melancholia I went out walking over the fields to Thorns Gill, where the rainwater was rushing noisily through that sudden cleft in the rolling drumlins at Ribblehead. The sheer irresponsibility of water flowing downhili, the nihilism of waterfalls and their anarchistic disrespect for rocks, are, in themselves, exhilarating. The rushing of underground rivers, hidden waters escaping from between the layers of the limestone at several levels, to join the white and foaming mainstream, caused the water to sing with many voices; but more joyful than all this noisy turbulence, quite silent, but glowing with inner life and promise of summers to come, were the rowan berries. Growing out and stooping down from the steep sides of the rocky watercourse, laden rowans dangled vermilion clusters over the water. They shone like coloured lights in that deep green landscape. Brighter than tomatoes or oranges on barrows in grimy streets, brighter than neon signs, they shone with a living brilliance made of the sunlight they have absorbed since they were blossoms. The summer is still present in these glowing berries, and in the rosehip rubies of the hedges, much as a poet still lives in his poems: and though, this morning — in the last week of September — there was cat ice on the puddles, and no bees on the still-undefeated comfrey flowers, I have, by feeding my eyes on rowanberry-light, regained my inner summer which, I hope, may keep me warm all winter.

Storm Gathering (1962)

The Hospitality of Rowan Trees

The summer-long slow burn of mountain ashes
prepares a feast. Light blossom-froth was starters,
but the main course, dragging the pliant twigs
earthward with heaviness, is berry-clusters
cooked to come-hither scarlet. Guests arrive.
Pot-shaped wood pigeons agitate the leaves
with flutterings and gluttony, and blackbirds
tabletalk and food-call, sotto voce,
while balancing on lithe unstable perches
and picking fruit precisely, with neat beaks.
They eat for weeks but do not strip the tree.
The starling squadrons do that in one day.
Gatecrashers spread the word, and avid flocks
pour out of nowhere, fill the tree with wings
and put an end to hospitality.

The festive baubles, painted by the sunlight
with many coats of colour as they grew:
green, brown, tan, orange, deeper orange, scarlet;
all luminous with warm ingested rays,
are lost, the feast for human eyes reduced
to tired and dowdy salad of green leaves.
This was not rape or theft but deed of gift;
not altruism either, but exchange.
The Rowan casts its bread upon the air—
red pellets gulped by gullets, crushed in crops—
in reciprocity. The tree provides
wages for seed-dispersing foresters
who feed, and scatter future Rowan trees.
Losing its life to save it, nature gives;
the principle is generosity.

Thistles

Thistles die in their prime. There is a poem which begins: 'The thistle now is older,/ His stalk begins to moulder,/ His head is white as snow.' But the common spear thistle doesn't allow itself to grow old at all; it dies fighting almost as soon as it has flowered. Its lowest leaves turn brown as the first flower comes out, and then death climbs, leaf by leaf, up its erect stem while it is in full bloom.

So, though in late summer the thistles are tufting the hillside pasture with beautiful purple flowers that no-one admires, by autumn they are nothing but the white haired corpses of plants — dead but not lying down. Upright to the last, their stiff-necked pride evokes associations with tragedy. In desiccated rags of leaves, with white hair blowing in the wind, they remind me of Lear on the heath. Later, in the first snow, these bleached multitudes become Bony's defeated army retreating from Moscow, with stiff necks broken, heavy heads nodding, emaciated stalks leaning sideways with exhaustion, and armour and weapons rusted; yet they aren't really beaten at all, but triumphant. Among them, next year's thistles are already starring the turf with their vegetable fortresses. They are not retreating but in possession, and they are building their speary castles faster by far than ever the Normans did in England. And they are building far more democratically. Every thistle's home is his castle; they have one each. Every thistle is his own baron, and only the grass is in serfdom — being severely taxed by cattle.

Old Jack Lambert who, amongst his other occupations and accomplishments, used to trap moles, once told me that he used to know a Methodist fellow who insisted that everything in creation has its use.

'What use are moles?' asked Jack, unconvinced.

'Drainage', answered the Methodist.

Maybe — but what use are thistles? They are the meaning and purpose of the universe to the thistle itself. It doesn't expect or desire to be useful to any external power. As far as thistles are concerned, God is a great ghostly thistle — infinitely spiky in Its concentric circles of defence against the grazing herds of Satan, and infinitely ingenious in facing Its weaponry in all directions at once. It turns the twisted edges of its leaves to sword after shining sword, as though it thrusts and parries continually in an eternal duel against vegetarian giants, and each time it makes a thrust a shining weapon crystallises in the air, and remains, as though there were no time, and all the battles of history are simultaneously present. Like any self-respecting god, he lives in eternity, and all of his manifestations are permanent.

Yet, in spite of the indifference of thistles concerning whether they are of service to anyone else, the goldfinches fly from one to another, contriving not to impale themselves on those unwelcoming needles, and they hollow out the brittle-scaled seedheads. For them a thistly hillside in the autumn sunshine is a fruitful field to be harvested.

A Cow Story

One autumn morning when I went into my studio after breakfast, I found it strangely dark. Something was blocking the light at the high window. Now my studio is a converted shippon, built into the side of a hill so that the floor is about six feet below ground level at the far end, where a small window pierces the thickness of the wall. Sheep and cows walk past this window, and often pause to peer down at me. In cold wintry weather, when the wind blows from the north-east, groups of sheep take shelter there, huddling together. Our cat also spies on me through this high window to assure herself that I am working hard to keep her in idleness.

On this particular morning there was something as massive as a wall between me and the light, and it seemed to be in no hurry to move. Completely shutting out the sky, it was as though a hairy double mattress stood on its side against the window, sagging slightly and breathing heavily. It was the flank of a pregnant cow, marked with big patches like maps of dark continents, as black as all the sorrows of the world. Black and white maps are the accepted uniform of cattle in our local fields: Asia or the Americas are worn over ribs, Australia on rumps, and Europe and its offshore islands on one shoulder, or slipping down a leg. I stared up at the heaving and slightly inaccurate map of Africa while, very slowly, like a more than usually inert stone rolling away from the entrance to a tomb, the cow moved away. I gave her little more thought after that, although I could hear her snorting, and occasionally bellowing, then mooing gently, quite close by. When the boys came in from school they asked if I would like to see a newborn calf.

'It's only just got up onto its feet', they said, 'it can't be an hour old.'

So I went outside and peered over the wall at a staggering, blunt-nosed bullcalf and its mother. The calf wore a map of the Isle of Wight and one or two random Channel Islands on its wet and curly hide. The mother licked it gently and nearly pushed it over, and mooed. So that was what she had been doing all day; that was what all the snorting had been about. We admired her work and praised her, then went indoors and forgot her.

It was late in the evening of the following day. We were returning from a visit to friends and we found our farmer neighbours, with waving torches, wandering about on our croft.

'We're looking for our cow that calved yesterday. We took the calf from her and she's that upset. We put her in a different field so she'd forget, like, but she's broken out and wandering, and she keeps returning to the place where she had it. Now we can't find her, and we're afraid she'll be out on t' road and she might cause an accident.'

At that moment the cow lurched round the corner of our house. We all combined to drive her out through our narrow gate into the field where she spent the night bellowing mournfully on the spot where she had given birth. Our neighbours, with raincoats on over their nightwear, for they had risen from bed to seek the cow, returned home, and again we forgot the poor bereaved mother whose instinct was stronger than it need be in a domesticated animal.

The following afternoon two black and white cows wearing the prescribed maps of imperfectly known worlds stood on the sunlit field and, side by side, contemplated a black and white object on the grass. It looked like a heap of discarded black and white clothes. It might have been the empty and crumpled skin of a piebald pantomime horse. One of the cows stepped forward and licked it cautiously. The other cow also licked it. They both stood very close to it and watched it intently. Was it breathing? Had it moved? The two cows took it in turns to lick it some more, and it stirred. It lifted a blunt-nosed calf's head on a wobbly neck and then folded itself up again. It was sleepy; it had just been through the very exhausting experience of being born. Its mother licked it tentatively. The other cow licked with enthusiasm. This cow wore a map of black Africa on her flank, and she was the very cow whose own calf had been stolen from her two days previously. Gently but firmly she was nudging the real mother away. As she licked the calf her swollen udder dripped white milk on the green grass. Within an hour the calf was hers, and the natural mother had accepted the situation.

'We wanted to sell her as a cow in milk', said her owners, a day later, 'but now she's too upset. She adopted that second calf, and when we took that one away as well she got upset all over again, but worse than before. We'll never get her to market now.'

We sympathised with our neighbours, but grieved for the cow; though not for long. This story has a happy ending.

'We'll have to give her a couple of calves to rear in a field', said the farmer, and I rejoiced for the cow. Yet I couldn't help considering that had she been a woman, running alive with hormones and aching to mother an infant, so that she stole another's child, human morality and legality would have condemned her.

Mists

This rolling green landscape could be Buckinghamshire — except for the stone walls, and the sparseness of the spindly trees — for none of our high peaks are visible. They are blotted out completely by a ceiling of low cloud, and might not be there at all. When the cloud drifts even lower, nearer ridges vanish, reappear, and vanish again. The hilltop wood becomes a faint grey silhouette. The sycamore by the lane is a shadow. The cow in the next field has become a rectangular block-like shape; it appears to have eight legs, but four belong to her calf, which is sucking.

In the foreground, which is almost all that is left of the view, berberis berries are ripening. They glow more incandescent every day, like coke in a furnace when the dampers are open. Rosehips are tattered by the attacks of birds, or soft and wrinkled with over-ripeness. Wild yellow poppies are still in bloom although it is October and they belong to May and June, and the rowan trees have been persuaded by the Indian summer to put out a few sprays of flower, as though it were spring.

Drops of water hang on fence-wires, on leaves and thorns and polished berries of the straggly bramble, which has hardly ever succeeded in ripening its fruit up here before. It grows too high up. This year there are still flowers on the laden sprays. Should this weather last until Christmas the blackberries would keep on coming.

But it is the mist that keeps coming now — washing out the landscape like a water-colour under the tap.

An invisible chaffinch sings his autumn song in the midst of an invisible hawthorn bush. He is the centre of his own globe of visibility, as we all are, and he can probably see dark green leaves, crimson berries, and not much else but whiteness beyond. A rook caws, quite close, and a shadow flaps by. The mist closes in, so I work indoors, trying to extend the sphere of my awareness inwardly, surrounded by the vanished world.

Going down to Settle later, when the mist has cleared a little, is like driving through a Chinese painting. The sun shines dazzlingly over Attermire, whose jagged top is dark against brightness. Bands of mist hide the hillside. A great cable of cloud hangs over the length of the Ribble, and Smearsett's pyramid-like top emerges from it unexplained. The river valley, for all we can see, might be an arm of the sea. Barns and trees appear as ghostly masses, as does the lumbering lorry ahead. The shade of a wide-winged, slow-flapping heron flies down-river through the mist; but the observation of birds from moving motor-cars, even at twenty miles per hour, is a dangerous habit. I must stop.

On clearer days the landscape is still a transformation scene. It seems that something is being hidden from us. The sun rises muffled and shrouded, like Lazarus from the tomb. Drifting clouds marble Pen-y-Ghent's darkness. The darkness presages rain. And after the rain the colour of the ashes can be seen to be slightly more gold. The copper beeches, fire-coloured in spring, have gone mud-brown. The dark cloud of leaves on the sycamore is wearing thin, and black tree-bones show through the culled foliage. Hedges are being shredded by the wind.

Something is afoot; the familiar vanishes everlastingly, and transformation follows transformation. Gauzes of mist, curtains of rain, trick lighting — spotlights of sun and haloed moons — are all tried in turn by the great scene-shifters. Illusion after illusion. They try everything but keep nothing for long; yet some new idea is emerging from the washes of mist and rain, and from the spasmodic shakings of the wind.

And the new idea, I begin to see, is November.

'Stop, Stop'

Now, more than at any other season, we would like time to stand still, or, if it must move — and that is its nature — to creep. For the trees are still beautiful in their fiery leaves, although some chestnuts, and the coarse leaved sycamores, strip early, and many a terminal ash tree leaf waves frantic goodbyes in the wind. So 'stay', we say to the autumn sunlight and the grass-of-parnassus flowers. 'Stay' we say to the October moon which is, as a three year old I used to know once said, 'broken already'; and 'stay' we say to the hare that leaps up from almost under our feet and rushes off without waiting to hear us. But nothing will stay.

Nevertheless, as each day becomes more beautiful than its predecessor, we would still detain the autumn if we could.

But Time has become a mad artist.

'Stop', we say, 'stop, that's lovely'; but it will not do for Time.

'No', he breathes, and blows all the golden leaves from the ash tree in a gale; and 'no' he mutters, picking away the scarlet berries from the rose-bush by means of bird-beaks. He flings fieldfares and redwings about the sky like flying seeds of winter. 'but it will not do', he sobs, scrubbing at his coloured canvas with violent, paint-stripping rains.

We go out early on the first morning after putting the clocks back. The wind is still dismantling the trees, and rain sighs gustily onto a strewn litter of leaves. Our car tyres hiss over their sodden carpet. Round a bend in the road we surprise a group of crows conducting an autopsy. They walk round solemnly, stabbing with black beaks into the fresh remains of a squashed hedgehog. It should be one of the last of this season's slaughters of sleepy hedgehogs by motorcars, for the month when one meets these animated hairbrushes at dusk, as they snuffle round the blackberry bushes where we are still gathering our sweet something-for-nothing, is all but over.

As we come home in the afternoon, it is already getting dark at four-thirty, and the dusk deepens rapidly as I go out walking for an hour, while potatoes bake.

In the trees above Douk Ghyll the wind is roaring louder than the waterfall below. The tall spindly trees rock with a circular movement as though they were stirring the porridgey-grey clouds above them, and their leaf-spotted branches flap up and down like wings. The brown leaves make a black pattern against the sky. The shadow of an owl flies silently and very fast through the trees, to disappear into the silhouette of a beech. I wait, hoping it may fly back, or be followed by another; but it has probably sensed my presence, and, in any case, nothing comes again.

I remember a pair of kestrels I saw flying in and out, and under and over, these same trees one bright day three weeks ago. From the corner of my eye I had thought, at first, that I saw brown pigeons. The wingbeat-speed is much the same. But, with wing-coverts conker-red in the sunlight, and long tails barred with black, they flew up and down this wooded beck several times, calling shrilly — *kek, kek, kek* — for a dramatic ten minutes. I don't know what this performance was all about, only that it will never come again, for nothing ever does. Nothing stays in nature, though sometimes we feel that we would like to keep everything; yet life is beautiful just because it changes, and autumn is so beautiful because it is a season of accelerating change, and sad because its changes dishevel and ruin the pride of the year.

Autumn Fires

The first smoulderings began in the great horse-chestnut tree by the beck, but the sycamores, the beeches and our few oaks soon glowed with their own yellow and orange fire. The hair on the larch turned gold with age, the hillside bracken rusted, and, as the rest of the landscape flared up for autumn, the horse-chestnut dropped its flames along with its few conkers and stood — charred and quite burnt out — though whole hillsides at Stainforth, Feizor and Austwick were still on fire with autumn.

One by one, leaves came spinning down out of the vicarage elms like dying birds, even when no wind blew. The trees grew threadbare so we could see the scaffolding of the woods, blotted with old rooks' nests in the high branches. Then the wind began to blow. Autumn blazed up brighter still, and the leaf-flames flew to the ground where they slowly grew dull and died. Robins flitted from bush to bush like brown sparks spreading the fire. Ash trees stripped themselves bare overnight, so their curving grey branches looked like beckoning bones against the darker woods. At night the roaring wind outside became a furnace with all its dampers open to consume the body of summer.

An undulating smoke of wind-blown rain passes over the valley — a procession of sighing ghosts through which we can see the hills. Rain hisses on the fire but cannot quench it. The woods roar like the sea. I think of the smoking waves breaking over the outer islands, and I am glad to be far inland. It is wild enough here.

On the 5th November it was calm, and we went out after dark for a bonfire-spotting walk. At first the only fire to be seen in the blackness was a white glow, veiled in pale smoke on the horizon to the east, where a half-moon struggled to rise in a caul of cloud.

Quite different were the red and smoky bonfires that soon erupted here and there about the valley, like volcanic pimples, while the broken disc of the moon lifted clear of Pen-y-Ghent.

An earthbound fire at Brackenbottoms flapped tatters of flame at the sky, and desperate sparks set off in hopeful migration heavenward. The heated air, eddying as it rose, and a light wind made the millions of flying sparks scribble a tangle of red-gold hair on the darkness. Rockets whooshed heavenward, to explode in momentary and expensive constellations, while beyond their brief mortality the stars shone white, still, and utterly remote.

But the stars are only still with a kind of motorway stillness. When, in a group of vehicles, we roar along at seventy miles per hour, we seem to be hovering still, although the disregarded landscape beyond the hard shoulder falls behind, as we remain in more or less the same relationship to our fellow roarers. So it is, I suspect, with ourselves and the stars. We have remained in the same relationship to them for so long that we are unaware of our headlong rush, together, through space and time to an unknown destination.

But the destination of autumn becomes all too apparent. On the morning after the Guy Fawkes fires we could see what it was that had been forged in the furnace of October.

The forests stand in ruins. Fieldfares are here already, perching among bare boughs. Colt Park Wood is a grey fuzz on its limestone ridge, though its blackthorns, now, are truly black. Park Fell casts its shadow there quite early in the afternoon, so darkness seems to lurk about all day. The wind blows cold from the north, and our fingers freeze; for it is winter.

Funereal Country Diary Note

In Memory of G B Butt (1963)

Through these mild, moist November weeks, though the overcast air has at times seemed laden with sooty darkness, black as the undertaker crows, and the dale to be in deep mourning, with the stripped copses showing as tear-smudged blotches on the drumlin hills, the herb-Robert has bloomed and bloomed on the moss-mortared walls, and here and there straggling survivors of the buttercup army have lingered. Garden primulas have produced spindly, sun-hungry flower stalks, and their buds have opened into disappointed cowslip-sized flowers, to discover death and the rigor mortis of frost.

Two mornings running, a dazzling sun has slowly thawed silver fields, stiff and shrivelled puddles, crunchy grass and cardboard washing. The scorn of the crows, and the built-in transistors of trippery starlings, tuned in to brief snatches of foreign music, were all that broke the silence, until a neuralgia-laden east wind came keening among the derelict larches. It seemed cold enough for snow when I went out today, but the wind, like a Chinese torturer, beat my face with invisible rods of icy rain, so that I half expected to be pockmarked. Now even the outer darkness seems to agree that home is the best place. It beats and shakes the windows, desperate to come in.

Once a Londoner

If a replica of Greater London were to be conjured into existence in Upper Ribblesdale, with Charing Cross where the Crown Inn now stands, it would cover this entire valley from Pen-y-Ghent's Plover Hill to Ingleborough's aerial football field. It would flow over these peaks and down their distant sides, swallowing Foxup and Arncliffe in one direction, and Clapham and Ingleton in the other. Its suburbs would reach as far as Kirkby Lonsdale to the west, and over Horsehead Fell to Hubberholme, and beyond, to the east. As far north as Dent and as far south as Bolton by Bowland, the earth would be covered with concrete and paving-stones, and Douk Ghyll, my favourite place, would be lost in a mish-mash of buildings, rush-hour traffic and city pigeons. The Houses of Parliament would sit heavily on Brackenbottoms. The Underground would go burrowing through the cave systems, and the becks would be tidily piped up and hidden away, as many of London's brooks are. Some of the streets would find themselves running up hills as steep as or steeper than stairs, but such perpendicular drops as the old quarry cliffs at Stainforth could be utilised to prop up towers of high-rise flats.

Though mountains and crags could not be levelled, woods and farmsteads certainly could. Concrete could be poured into the grykes up on the limestone pavements, shopping precincts and car-parks could be made there. Yet, horrible though this vision is, there have been times, I am ashamed to admit, when I have wished it could happen. These times have usually been in November, when the world pitches downhill into rapidly darkening winter, and I have been overwhelmed by a feeling I can only name as Exile. I have wished, treacherously, that London could plant its heavyweight self in this silent and empty country. For 'once a Londoner always a Londoner', as the Brixton woman who came here as an evacuee at the beginning of the war, and who stayed on to work and marry here, says, from time to time, in her Yorkshire accent that is built on a still obvious foundation of cockney.

I think it is the silence of November that provokes this mood. If I go outside it is into a grey and silent world. The fields are blurred by mists, and the mountains erased. An unseen sheep coughs, consumptively, somewhere out in the mist, underlining the silence. A crow flaps past, scanning the ground for carrion. There is an occasional flopping sound, of saturated ash tree leaves falling heavily to the ground. Rooks walk about a nearby field, solemn as undertakers. But nothing is happening, not even a funeral. The trees are weeping silently, for nothing. Our chickens are huddled and silent under a hedge of straggly bushes. Their hutches and sheds, built by the boys, appear depressingly slummy. They have nothing at all to do with architecture, and I think again of London.

I remember the early mornings of the Battersea years, waking to hear the gradually mounting rumble of the traffic with a sense that a great organism was waiting and stirring itself into motion with me. Perhaps it was a vast and intricate machine, its energy generated by the rush, bustle and competition of its population. And this population was by no means exclusively human. Our flat alone had pigeons in the roof and mice in the walls. When our first child was born we had to put his carry-cot up on a coffee table at night, so that the mice would not run over him as he slept.

I think of the alarm-notes of blackbirds as a typical London noise, although blackbirds are to be found everywhere, even here. I remember the evening scream-up of roosting starlings; the morning murmurings of the pigeons who lived in our roof; the afternoon shouting of newsboys about late night finals (from about midday onwards); and the hiss of tyres over shining wet roads; the cornflakey crunch of plane tree leaves on pavements; the jokey bus conductors; the dong of the bell for starting and stopping the bus; the rattle of underground trains, and their high-pitched brakes as they slow down to stop; and the incessant, indescribable noise of people. It is the people that are the attraction. The gravitational pull of millions against Horton's few hundreds seizes me as it seizes so many people in underpopulated places, thus making the underpopulation worse. So we arrange to spend the November half-term week in London.

Of course, having arranged it, we wish we weren't going. 'Do we really have to leave now?' we groan, as the last trees turn more golden, and the beeches, in particular, are just on the point of reaching their maximum splendour. The wood at Douk Ghyll is a vivid tapestry — orange, red, brown, purple, yellow-greens — hanging before the grey, steeply tilted fields of Pen-y-Ghent side. It seems to hover, like a mirage. 'Only for a few days', we say, bidding farewell to our low, grey stone cottage which turns its back on the north wind and the winter. Nowadays I don't have the courage to say the word 'goodbye', I use the ambiguous 'see-you', an optimistic charm against the hazards of the motorway. I realise that this is a frailty, like other superstitions, but there it is. Then we burn time and petrol travelling south to camp for a week in the house of a friend, between a roaring road and the stinking river, and under the flight paths made inaudible by the road.

Of course we had a very interesting time, and we saw a lot of art galleries and visited friends, and of course it was worth it — but when I return I find that the one week of my absence has stripped all the trees. It will be a whole year before I can see those burning bushes again. I have missed the climax of autumn, and it is total winter here now. The hovering tapestry of green, orange and purple at Douk Ghyll was, after all, an illusion, as I suspected all along: everything is black and grey there now.

'For what have I sold this week?' I ask myself, and then remember the greenish gold of the plane trees in Russell Square. I remember the maps of greens and greys that pattern their bark. I remember the Greek Nereids in the British Museum; I am thinking still what a time it must have been when men first discovered that they could make the human spirit live in stone, and persuade the breath of life to flow through that dense material, so that the stone appeared to move. I remember pearly London skies, framed in jagged roof-shapes. I remember the river, for all its aroma, satin smooth, with reflected lights of Hammersmith Bridge stabbing deep into its darkness. Hammersmith Bridge itself, that beautiful, anachronistic traffic-jammer; and, over the midnight streets, the moon, already almost half full, and fuzzed with mist. The same moon that shines over Horton or the Hebrides. 'Beauty is everywhere', I tell myself, seeing — deep in the most sheltered heart of the wood at Douk Ghyll — a sycamore with golden leaves like a caged fire behind the dark bars of the bare trees; but home is here, though conversation and easy-going chatter may be in London.

I read somewhere the story of a man who dreamed that if he travelled an immense distance — perhaps it was to Prague — he would meet, on a certain bridge, a man who would tell him where a priceless treasure lay hidden. So he made the long journey to Prague (if it was Prague) and there, on the designated bridge, he met a man who told him that under the hearthstone of his distant home, a priceless treasure was buried.

I resume my laborious digging for treasure, at home, which is where one works.

I remember my treasonable fantasy of a second London built here, in Upper Ribblesdale, and it appears to me now like a spotlessly new Ordnance Survey map, spread before my mind's eye, with all its intricate detail of contour lines and symbolic crags and bright green patches for woods, and tinily written place-names that no-one has ever heard of, upon which I had deliberately spilt the coffee, or dropped a rag soaked in sump oil, so that a greasy stain creeps over it, obscuring all its fine print of coppices, farmsteads, fern-filled grykes and crinkled threads of becks. Sowerthwaite, Nappa Scars, Norber Brow, Dearbought Plantation, Birch Show Rocks, Winterscale, Hailshower Fell, Cold Stone Plain and Upper Sheepwash; all these evocative names disappear under the dark grey that symbolises a maze of deep streets to disguise the contours of the land. This is what was done, in reality, to the watermeadows by the Thames at Battersea in the nineteenth century. This is what happened to London's Clapham, and Camberwell. Some of our Yorkshire contours would take a lot of disguising. High crags would have to be left bare, as they are in Edinburgh, but one London is quite enough, even with differences. It was not really London that I was pining for: it was youth — forever lost. Not the light-footed energy and consciousness of the power of my own good looks, but the illusions; the hope, ambition, faith in one's own talents, and the expectation that doors will simply fly open at one's approach. (Some of them did, but usually for the wrong reasons.)

Now, having eaten a great deal of the humble pie of life, I am left with the labour of justifying those early ambitions. With a pen for a trowel, I should dig under my own hearthstone as carefully as an archaeologist, sifting for objects and examining each fragment that I find with close attention, though not necessarily in order to look backwards.

Mountains and Clouds 2 (1961)

Un-news for a Local Paper

In Horton-in-Ribblesdale rain is scarcely news. 'Come to Horton and get lovely and brown with rust', is a rather well-worn local joke. Even floods at Horton are not news — although the grey Ribble water spread out over the fields, the racing becks rushing down to swell the thundering falls at Stainforth via the rapids below Sherwood Brow, and the white water roaring from the darkness of Douk Ghyll cave (as though something vital has burst in the plumbing of Pen-y-Ghent), are all dramatic enough to seem like news. The truth is that this back-cloth to our lives up here is really grander than petty human affairs, newsworthy though they may sometimes be.

The past week has been drowned in gusty rain, and the fields were flooded more often than not, and while the tail of the weekend gale was still lashing the stripped trees and making newly washed clothes dance wildly on washing lines, I went out to discover that most of the floods have gone down; but that can hardly be news if the floods themselves were not news. The river was contained within its banks again, though silver pools lay here and there on the fields. Most of the trees were now quite bare, but the beckside larches were still golden. They dangled naked flood-washed roots in the water. Each flood also licks soil from under the river-bank grass so as to leave it hanging over the edge in little mats.

Caverns among exposed roots by the water make a paradise for wrens, who flit in and out of their many-windowed mansions. They are pleased, perhaps, with enlarged quarters. But the pleasure of wrens, a little more soil erosion, and a few boughs broken from trees by the wind do not amount to a news item. Even a whole fallen tree is not newsworthy, unless it blocks a road. But patches of light planing down the far-away slopes of Park Fell, racing towards us and dazzling us for a moment, then moving on to floodlight Pen-y-Ghent, are the first rays of sunshine we have seen for a week, and surely, though not news, that is good news.

Tortoiseshells Overwintering

In my bedroom ceiling's shadiest corner
a dark encampment of inverted tents
is sitting out the tyranny of Winter.

Like Israelites that keep God's covenants
in sober arks, or nomad bedouins
who hide rich mats in fustian tenements,

they fold the magic carpets of their wings,
concealing hieroglyphics of the meadow
clapped between tatter-bordered coverings.

As dingy as the withered nettlebed,
as drab as marbled bibles, charred by fire,
or chips of bark or stone, they could be dead

but hang by wiry legs, as fine as hair,
close-clustered near the plaster desert's edge
like a proscribed religious sect at prayer.

This bivouac preserves the Summer's page
during eclipse of dandelions and daisies;
it bears pressed sparks of sun through this dark age:

one night between oasis and oasis.

Moorland. Head of Littondale (1960)

First Snow

In nature nothing — except perhaps an earthquake — ever happens with dramatic suddenness. Our children do not suddenly start talking, but they practise sounds for months before they utter even single words, nor do they get up out of their prams and walk in one day, but crawl, and stand about holding on, keeping us in expectation, long before they take their first few unsupported steps. Art begins tentatively, and fame grows from an almost inaudible rumour. War, fortunately, never begins with the suddenness of a clap of thunder, but there are rumblings, groanings and border skirmishes beforehand to warn us; and so it is with the seasons. Winter does not arrive in frost and icicles overnight, nor spring burst out in buds and birdsong one morning, but there is much overlapping. Remnants of autumn cling to the trees in March, first signs of spring appear in January (before the winter has really got underway), and there is always the perverse ivy that reverses the seasons by blooming in autumn and bearing its berries in the spring.

This year, especially, summer lingered on through autumn. Honeysuckle, its flowers shrinking smaller and smaller, bloomed throughout September, and all through October those wild yellow poppies that belong to May, June and July, were still opening. Ferns, even now, are still green, and in the woods the leaves turned colour late and hung on long.

Yet a few days of gale can strip the trees of all but a few surviving leaves, and transform the forests from gold and green to black. But the black is an illusion. The woods are really green with the moss that enjoys its summer in the winter, and grey-blue with lichens, if we look closely. The newly naked twigs themselves have their own colours. They may appear, from a distance, like a black lace trimming along the horizon, but it is a black mixed from many colours. The ash twigs are grey-green and still carry bunches of rusty keys which they may send, in the next gale, to open the gates of the ground to release other ash trees. The twigs of our slow growing lime tree, which doesn't really like the climate of its mountainside situation, are red and pliable, the buds clumsy and club-like, unlike the bronze-coloured beech buds which taper like fine Chinese paint brushes. And they all draw different and individual signatures on the November sky. Larches are knobbly with blunt round buds, like French knots, and plum-tree twigs are kinky and crumpled like tangled embroidery thread that has been pulled out in the undoing of a particularly unsuccessful piece of stitchery. Birches are reddish, and draw delicately on the sky. Blackthorns really are black, and spikier than barbed wire at its most paranoid. They look like suffering itself, and make a crown of thorns for the limestone walls and the crags. Remaining sloes are blue. Hawthorn trees are also spiky, but less so than the blackthorn, and purple with berries. Fieldfares sit among them, refugees from a harder winter than ours.

Yet even here it has turned very cold, and late at night the light from our uncurtained window shines on a hesitatingly falling dust of snow. It is settling on the ferns and making a filigree of white among the twigs and branches in the garden. In the morning the fields appear to have aged overnight. They have gone grey as though they have received dreadful news on the north wind; and Pen-y-Ghent has its crags picked out in white lines, while Whernside wears a white cape.

It isn't very much snow — though we hear of more on the East Coast — but it's a beginning. And in nature nothing ever happens with dramatic suddenness. This is just the title page, or perhaps the preface, to the book full of great white pages of snow to come.

Brother Fox

Men net the seeming-docile hills
in mesh of walls, but fail
to kill the fox of the high fells
who lives beyond the pale.

I trickle under drystone walls
while staid law-keepers dream,
and creep, when mooncast shadow falls,
towards the valley farm.

The serpent writhes in my backbone,
the snake dances in yours,
and treacherously lets me in
to snap my wanton jaws.

Men load the valley fields with walls
but still cannot subdue
the bandit of the stony fells
who lives, deep-earthed, in you.

I trot, blood-dark, close by the wall,
under snow-smothered moon,
printing bad news with each footfall
towards the winking town.

The serpent writhes in my backbone,
the snake dances in yours,
and hypnotises gentle men
into bloodlust and wars.

The Wars of White and Brown

Obliterating green, white claims the field;
it stole in overnight.
The world grows moralised and mineral,
but Harry, the commander of the grass —
including flesh — drives tractors out to fight.
His vandal muckspreader bombards the snow
with warm and odoriferous manure.
He leads the loaded weapon up and down
leaving a scribbled page — 'Long live dark gut:
cattle survive on silage, last year's green
which shall be green again. Organic rules!'
He scrawls war-slogans on the snow with shit.

But the North-East sends days and nights of snow.
The air is thick with bullets. Polar bees
sting faces. When the white invasions cease,
and smoke of battle clears,
the lanes are blocked, gates locked, by drifts.
The tractors cannot reach ice-armoured fields.
So farmers fight with spades, and tumble walls
to take baled rations to their starving troops.
Shabby guerrilla armies rally round
hay-trailers, running from white distances;
ragged and dirty in a sinless world
of inorganic crystal innocence.

Then milder air breathes brown holes in white fields;
dark patches spread like spillage, grow to seas
eroding capes and bays of arctic land.
Brown rivers swell with blood of wasted snow
till ice returns to check this haemorrhage
and the North-east brings wave on wave
of six-limbed entities, each one to fall,
so dresses hills with stifling bandages
and sterile winding-sheets of snow.

But hero Harry's army from the farm
breaks through, relieves the bleating garrisons,
and clears the lanes again.
Brute tractors violate the virgin field.
Berserk, the scatological machine
flings dung, and docile tanks, led up and down,
pour cattle-urine, pumped from shippon drains,
to scent and stain the snow.
Harry has such reserves of weaponry,
though fields lie frozen, and small privates die.
The redcoat robin and civilian wren
have lost the battle now. Condemned to live,
black widow rooks grieve up and down the field,
feeding on seeds in dung. Clown hare lies dead,
armed to his radar ears with cowardice;
and when it seems that skewbald hills grow green,
the north wind brings white armies in again.

So to and fro the battle goes — now brown
then white, then brown again. Shrill cries
of prematurely born, pipecleaner lambs
are quickly stilled. Reconnaissance of larks
retires, discouraged. Lapwing pioneers
shriek 'Victory!' Advance, retreat, advance;
till light-buds glimmer on the blacked-out thorn
and curlew calls a truce.
The quivering pennants of the green-tongued earth,
unanimously mute, declare the peace.

A Christmas Card

This is rather an expensive Christmas card. It costs about ten pence a week to keep our robin so round and our blackbird so sleek, but if we didn't put out food for them the full-colour, three-dimensional moving picture of birds feeding outside the kitchen window would assemble elsewhere to devour someone else's ten-penny-worth. This munificence is pure luxury on our part for — except in very severe weather — food for wild birds isn't really necessary. Our landscape is made of bird food, and if it weren't the birds wouldn't stay. They have wings. Now, in mid-December, we have flocks of visiting fieldfares and redwings from the far north to help our native birds to eat up their plenty, and still the hedges are full of hips and haws. In our garden a briar bush is still laden with vermilion berries that shone out against the snow a few weeks ago, and yet remain uneaten.

In that same brief cold spell I was out one afternoon, walking among the trees near Douk Ghyll. The tree-boles were luminously green in the nearly horizontal sunshine. Beyond them the snow was striped with their blue shadows. It was very cold, and the ground was frozen hard. There was neither sight nor sound of animal life among the trees, except for the spidery blots of old rook's nests in the high branches, and the wind was still, as though it had died in the cold air. Yet in the midst of this perfect silence, which only I had broken, I heard a footfall; and then another, and another. They came at irregular intervals. A step, and a step; and a step. But there was no-one to be seen. I felt that an invisible man was abroad, or jokey children were prowling and hiding behind the trees. There was another footstep, and another. Then I saw the source of these sounds — a blackbird was hopping over the drifts of leaves. It stopped, and with its beak it rummaged among the leaves at its feet, found something — a large and edible treasure, a worm, perhaps, or a beetle — shook, and swallowed it. He had no need of our offerings of seeds, nuts, and cheese-parings. This cold and stony earth in which we would starve without grocery shops, is home and mother to him. So it is really for our own pleasure that we spread our charitable table. Yet the blackbird who first found it was, to begin with, very possessive of this miraculous food hoard. He became so busy guarding it that he had no time to eat it.

He chased away the robin and greenfinches that kept on arriving, but now he is accustomed to the self-renewing plenty, and is more tolerant of his rivals.

They are, mainly, one robin, several greenfinches and chaffinches, many bluetits, great-tits and tree-sparrows, and one, I think, dunnock, which is not really anyone's rival. Its behaviour matches its quiet slatey-grey and brownish plumage, and it is content with the crumbs that fall from the table. As for the wrens, they flit about the saxifrage and mosses on the walls, probing for insects and taking nothing from us. The bluetits divide their time between a bag of nuts and the assorted scraps, darting about from one to the other with their characteristic quickness. They move with the jerky rapidity of a very old film. To our eyes the intermediate stages of their movements are missing. To watch one is like flicking through one of those books of pictures of a figure in various stages of an action, such as we used to make as children. But if they appear quick to us, how slow we must appear to them — cumbersome as clouds in our slow-motion driftings. We must seem to grope through a thicker air, driven by a numb and dreaming brain.

The animated Christmas card becomes very expensive indeed when the starlings find it. They come like coach parties to a small wayside inn, and eat up all our stock. Though so numerous, they are not to be despised as vermin, though I do sometimes wonder why it is that we get so much pleasure out of feeding birds and none out of feeding rats and mice. I suppose it is because food for the birds is a gift, while food for the mice is a theft. Besides, the birds remain outside.

It pleased me to find recently that W H Hudson loved starlings, and for his shepherd friend they were a favourite bird. Flocks of starlings associate with sheep, and in some areas are often to be seen riding on their backs and pecking parasites from their fleeces. W H Hudson's shepherd said that starlings would take refuge among sheep, falling into the flock 'like a shower of stones', if a sparrow-hawk was about. They would remain hidden about the feet of the sheep until danger was past.

Hudson is very observant and analytical about their song. I am always grateful to them for singing all the year round, and reminding me of the long warm days when the air is full of music. Hudson's starlings, among their other mimicries, included the sound of sheep-bells, of which they would have heard a lot in those days. Hudson points out that they need not all have heard the bells for themselves, for they would all imitate each other (as we do), as well as record direct experience of external nature.

But I don't think starlings are still imitating their parents imitating their grandparents, imitating their more distant forebears imitating the sheep-bells of former times, for our starlings imitate telephone bells. I have been deceived, more than once, into running into the house to find it full only of silence, with starling-song outside.

If starlings were rare we would praise their iridescent beauty more than we do. One flew into one of our windows and killed itself the other day, and I went out to pick it up at once, so that at first its plumage was alive with coloured jewels; but all its fires went out as it died, leaving it still beautiful, but merely speckled. Their sociable habits, too, have a beauty of their own. Whole flocks whirr up from the ground and leap from field to field like a collective grasshopper. Their amoeba-like flocks that fly as one organism continually changing its amorphous form, are a common but wonderful sight. I used to watch them while waiting for buses at Piccadilly in Manchester; and the pouring of flock upon flock of starlings through Manchester's evening sky, converging to roost in the trees of an island in the lake at Platt Fields, in what must have been millions of shrilly screaming birds, is another of my memories of that city.

But while I have been thinking about starlings in general, twenty or thirty particular starlings have eaten up all our bird food, which must be replenished if we are to maintain our expensive, living Christmas card.

The Christmas Tree

Every year we buy a small fir tree, with a root, from Settle market, and welcome it and its scent of fir woods into the house a day or two before Christmas. The children decorate it, which, in my opinion but not theirs, makes it look somewhat less rather than more beautiful, and they become very Christmassy about it. Mysterious wrapped presents are put beneath it, and not allowed to be touched. The tree becomes the guardian of gifts.

After a day or two, the coniferous fragrance that the tree brought in with it becomes less noticeable — either because we have grown used to it or else because the little green being, in its crêpe-paper-wrapped bucket of earth, wearing tinsel baubles and tawdry crown, is suffocating in the indoor heat. I begin to feel very sorry for it, and can almost hear it gasping for breath and feel its longing for the mid-winter wind. It would so very much prefer to be out of doors in a day-long downpour of grey rain, or to be frozen, and perhaps to have ice crystals growing on it, or to be laden with snow instead of all this rainbow finery. It would like to be in total darkness all night, or under the glitter of the stars, and not to suffer unnatural lights and the dangerous proximity of fire. The Christmas tree seems to suspect its own inflammability. It scatters needles, like green hairpins, in distraught dehydration.

As soon as is decently possible after Christmas — long before Twelfth Night — we take the sacrificial tree outside and plant it; but it is eloquent of the deadly nature of home comforts for fir trees that, out of quite a number, only three have survived. One is now quite large — being the tallest member of my family by a good head, and, as it can be seen from the kitchen and living-room windows, we have made it into a kind of Christmas tree for the birds.

When the severe weather begins, we decorate it with nets of nuts, millet sprays, chunks of suet and old mutton bones left over from the weekly cannibal feast that is a traditional part of British family life; so the tree, of its own accord, becomes decorated with bluetits, great-tits, robins, sparrows, dunnocks, greenfinches, chaffinches, occasional blackbirds and periodic starling hordes. The tree can be rocking in a gale, its branches gesturing desperately in the wind and the bag of nuts swinging like a pendulum, yet a bluetit will arrive with the suddenness of the demon king in a pantomime, bounce onto the green trampoline branches, clean its beak on the twig between its feet, and jump onto the nut bag and eat the meal. Simply to watch can make a human feel queasy; but birds must be immune to seasickness.

Our Christmas-tree-for-the-birds has lived close to us for several years now, so we have seen it through all its seasons more than once. It becomes decorated by frost and snow, and by pendent waterdrops when snow and ice are melting. It seems happy to have its lower limbs weighed to the ground by snow, and to be comfortably cold in its polar coat of ice-crystals in prolonged frost. It can, and often does, drip countless disappearing diamonds in a day-long drizzle. It looks very beautiful in all these forms of decoration, and it seems to be keeping itself very fit in the wind; but it is most beautiful in May when it adorns itself with bright green tufts of brand-new needles. Each small green shaving-brush pushes off the conical hat that was once the casing of its bud, and expands in the sunshine. Soon it becomes impossible to imagine how such a great brush could have been packed into this tiny cap. The tree loves the natural warmth of the sun, and it sweats a fragrant gum. The sun is not like the central heating that slowly cooked it, or the fire that scorched and dried it. Under its influence the new green grows, giving proof that the tree is alive and well, and has forgiven us the ordeal by Christmas.

Shepherds' Carol

1st Shepherd

As I came wayfaring
over the barren stones
I heard a secret spring
that carolled in clear tones:
'I am earth's child, I sing
let me be a plaything
For Mary's child.' I bring
As gift, this singing water.

2nd Shepherd

As I walked on the dead
Grass of the tawny fells,
I saw beneath my tread
These meek, white snowdrop bells
Which prayed — 'Don't crush my head,
But pluck me from this bed
And take as a shy bride
For God's son, Winter's daughter.'

Shepherd Boy

As I ran through the frost
That blossomed on the ground,
I heard a shrill redbreast
Singing — 'The thawing wind
Is locked in my bright chest:
Hear now sweet Summer's sound
Threading the pillared forest.'

I chased but never caught her
So bring the joy I thought her
In both my empty hands.

About the Author and the Artist

Anna and Norman Adams met as teenagers at Harrow Junior Art School during the Second World War.

Anna has worked as an art teacher, designer and freelance artist, and she does still exhibit, but writing has gradually become her principal work. Previous publications are mainly of poetry: *A Reply to Intercepted Mail,* 1979; *Brother Fox,* 1983; *Dear Vincent* and *Trees in Sheep Country*, 1986; *Angels of Soho*, with pictures by Norman Adams, 1988; and *Nobodies*, 1990. In 1991 came *Island Chapters*, which is mainly prose, but with some poems, and eight pictures by Norman Adams. *Life on Limestone* follows the same pattern, but is a gathering together, in seasonal order, of writings inspired by her surroundings in Upper Ribblesdale.

Norman Adams has devoted his life to painting. He has exhibited regularly in London since 1952, and also in many other parts of Britain. He has works in the Tate Gallery in London and other public collections. He was elected ARA in 1967, and full RA in 1972. Watercolours from nature have always been an important part of his *oeuvre*, but his major works are imaginative compositions, often of a religious, philosophical or poetic nature. He has had several important public commissions; the latest work in progress is a sequence of fourteen stations of the cross for the 'Hidden Gem' — St Mary's Roman Catholic Church in central Manchester.